WORKING WOMEN AND RELIGION

WORKING WOMEN AND RELIGION

Dr. B. SUGUNA
Dept. of Women's Studies
Sri Padmavathi Mahila Viswa Vidyalayam
TIRUPATI

Discovery Publishing House
NEW DELHI-110002
(INDIA)

First Published 1994

Reprinted-2011

ISBN 81-7141-245-9

Published by

DISCOVERY PUBLISHING HOUSE
4831/24, Ansari Road, Prahlad Street
Darya Ganj, New Delhi-110002 (India
Phone: 23279245 • Fax: 91-11-23253475
E-mail:dphtemp@indiatimes.com

Printed at Mehra Offset Press, Delhi

Foreword

It is a general belief that education brings about improvement in the status of women which enables them to see traditional practices and customs with a new scientific approach. This enables them to redefine culture and religion and make it a mere meaningful phenomenon in their lives. But, mere education will not bring about the required results. The improvement in their economic status will have a strong influence on their attitude towards religious practices and beliefs.

Compared to India and other developing countries in the South-East Asian regions, the developed countries thus far have given less importance to religious beliefs and practices. This is not merely due to cultural values, but mere due to the practical problems faced by women who have to divide the twenty-four hours for multifarious activities in the home and work place. Total negligence of religion has also resulted in other types of social problems like drug addiction, alcoholism, incestual behaviour and the like.

The present work which mainly focuses on the attitudinal changes in the religious practices and beliefs among working women is a research work done by Dr. (Mrs.) B. Suguna in the field of Sociology. Though a large number of studies on women have come into existence which have invariably dealt with various dimensions of women's life in a routine manner, the present study is interesting as it has thrown substantial light upon the religious beliefs and practices of working women.

The study within the context of religion has far-reaching implications because the changes witnessed and noted seemed to have a lasting effect on the life of working women and also influence their children's attitudes. For the present work, the authoress has chosen Tirupati as the area of study for her own obvious reasons. The sample consists of different socio-economic set-ups and religious and caste compositions. Hence, the study is fairly a representative in character, the results of which would be true for many other places in the country since the status of women all over India is almost the same except for a few specific differences which are more of a degree than a concept.

The authoress could have dealt far more deeply into the life and thinking of working women in the field of religion by taking some more variables and aspects and their impact on the society. A deeper insight into some more aspects would have thrown more light and revealed some curious facts. In spite of this lacuna, the work is a good attempt in this area. The study, as I view it in a broader way, is a bold venture attempted by the authoress. The work itself is explorative and thought-provoking. It is undoubtedly a significant contribution to the field of Women's studies. And I wish and foresee that this work would be a source of inspiration for greater studies on the life of working women, and will be beneficial to all the social scientists who have taken keen interest in women's development and progress.

Dr. K.A. PARVATHY
Professor & Head, Dept. of
Women Development Studies,
University College,
Sri Padmavati Mahila Viswavidyalayam,
Tirupati.

Preface

The changing status and position of women in India is an important field for research in this country and a subject of great interest in other countries today. Significant studies on women have been made in India from time to time. Innumerable books and research articles have been published on various dimensions of social, political, economic and cultural problems confronted by women. The subject still draws a great deal of attention from sociologists in particular and economists, political scientists, legal experts and others in general and it continues to be for many hundreds of years to come.

In view of the various studies made by scholars, two important developments with regard to the changing status of women in India may be taken into perspective. On the one hand, despite the Constitutional safeguards and social legislations passed to improve the status of women, women in India cannot be regarded as being emancipated from the old traditions and customs detrimental to the flowering of their personalities. More and more women have been entering educational institutions, professions and public life. Nonetheless, the position, status and condition of the mass of Indian women, however, remain more or less unchanged in the reality of their daily lives. There is a great hiatus, indeed as untruth, that divides the political vocabulary from the beliefs, customs and traditions of most Indians, ranging from the upper class down to the lowest class. Even today, the majority of women live in perpetual subservience, self-denial and self-sacrifice.

Hence, the need is for total emancipation of women from the clutches of traditions and customs and male-dominated society. What is required is that the socio-economic conditions of the teeming Indian women in the rural areas have to be improved a lot. The problems confronted by Indian women are multi-dimensional and therefore, a multi-dimensional approach and solutions will have to be applied for their uplift. No society can develop fully without a significant contribution by women towards its development. It is the men and women can create a democracy. It is further realised that harmony between the two sexes is a pre-requisite for the harmonious development of society. This is possible through creating an awareness by means of education which itself is the half the process of development in a developing society. Unless such an awareness is celebrated in the form of positive action, the process of development will be still-born.

On the other hand, in the light of several changes, social, political, economic and cultural aspects of women's life, the changing Indian woman is caught between two extremities, the traditional pattern of society and the advancing Westernised modern society. Hindu women have been highly traditional since the times of Vedic age. The cultural heritage of India was passed from generation to generation through the help of women. The women of India were brought up in a severe and rigid tradition bound by sanctions and invisible penalties which made them adhere with deliberate care to what their elders had passed on to them. Hindu tradition, bound up with domestic rituals, customs and practices, was held together mainly by women. This provided the basis of family and community life and strengthened group mores. The impact of alien influences on them could greatly undermine their faith in traditional norms and values. Even today, she remains to be more or less traditional in her outlook and as far as her social and cultural life is concerned despite she herself is in great transition.

It may be noticed that in view of her being traditional in thinking and action, Indian woman is not able to escape the influence of modern ways of living and thought. In the process of modernisation, many educated Indian women are slowly cultivating the modern patterns of behaviour. It is in this process of transition that she is not able to assimilate the conflict between the traditionalism and modernity. Though she is adopting the modern thoughts and ways, it may be seen that the traditional value system have not been clearly eroded by the modernisation. As the sociological studies in the cultural India show values are still preserved and safeguarded from the onslaughts of modernisation. That Indian women are fundamentally committed to certain moral principles that are part of Indian cultural heritage. Whatever the conclusion may be drawn, the vehement question is how to adopt beneficial aspects of another culture without being affected by its injurious aspects. And it also remains to be seen to what extent the traditional Hindu values will be preserved, adhered and practised in the context of changing Indian society.

It is against this background, the present study has been made. The main purpose of this study is to find out to what extent religious rituals and practices are adhered and followed by 300 educated working women which include 271 Hindus, 21 Christians and 8 Muslims and also try to see whether or not they still retain them in view of the several changes that crept into the domain of woman's life which altered her position and status in the society. The study is confined to Tirupati town in Andhra Pradesh. The greater emphasis and stress however is laid on the changes among 271 Hindu working women.

The major finding of the study is that the working women still have faith and belief in essential religious tenets such as the existence of God, harmony of all religions, the divinity of soul, the creation of universe by God, the theory of transmigration of soul and religion the basis for a true way of life, though certain changes are visible in their attitude towards religious rituals, customs and practices in their day-to-day life. The changes are however viewed as peripheral and not deeper.

It is now my duty to place on record my deep sense of gratitude to my guide late Professor A. Satyanarayana Murthy, M.A., Ph.D., for his kind and able supervision of this work and his constant and ready encouragement, but for whose kind help, untiring enthusiasm and valuable guidance, this work could have been neither conceived nor completed nor have seen its print.

Several research scholars and friends were very helpful in bringing the overall work to fruition. I owe a great debt of gratitude to them. The three hundred working women including 271 Hindus, 21 Christians and 8 Muslims were another source of inspiration and encouragement for me. When I approached them with questionnaires, they readily and whole heartedly supplied information without fear and doubts for my work. I benefitted a great deal from them. I am immensely thankful to them.

I am sincerely obliged to the Staff of S.V. University Library who readily supplied me the vast mass of literature I needed from time to time. The S.V. University generously granted me fellowship for two years from 1981 to 1983. The ICSSR also provided me a short term fellowship for three months to carry out my field work. I acknowledge their assistance with gratitude.

I am highly grateful to Professor K.A. Parvathi, M.A., Ph.D., Professor and Head, Department of Women's Studies, Sri Padmavati Mahila Viswavidyalayam, Tirupati who has graciously and unhesitantly accepted to write foreword to this book. For her critical observations, kind and encouraging words and unstinted moral support she has rendered, I ever remain indebted.

While recording feelings of appreciation and gratitude for many, I should not forget my husband Dr. J. Pratap Reddy who not only initiated me into this field of study but sustained my interest and enthusiasm all along. I am extremely grateful to him.

Dr. (Mrs.) B. SUGUNA

Contents

1

Introduction

Religion—Meaning And Definition

According to the *Dictionary of the Social Sciences*, the term "Religion" is derived from the Latin verb "Religere" which means the conscientious fulfilment of duty, awe of higher powers, deep reflection. Religion is a system of belief in supernatural power, which is usually acknowledged to be superhuman, who can influence material events and human life. Religion is a systematic patterns of beliefs, practices, values and religious behaviours acquired by man as a member of society. Such learning is both conscious and sub-conscious. These are as old as human thought. They are the living relics of thoughts much older than our own, and of religious beliefs and practices once strongly held, but now abandoned and forgotten to a large extent. According to Radford and Radford the present day superstitions are fragmentary remains of forgotten faiths, rituals and systems of thought, left behind when these faded from human minds (Radford, E. and Radford M.L., 1969 : 7). It is generally believed that primitive and uneducated people are mostly religious, some highly equcated people are also prone to many superstitious beliefs and ritual practices.

Religion supports the entire structure of religious beliefs and ritual practices. Religion satisfies some psychological needs for human beings. It fosters many superstitious beliefs such as the curses of some evil spirits, belief in omens, magic, etc. Religious beliefs are not just a primitive phenomenon. They are widespread in scientifically advanced societies as will. Notwithstanding remarkable expansion of general knowledge and great advances of science and technology, religious beliefs and practices continue to persist in people's lives. Most of the cultures encourage people to acquire beliefs in the existence of beings and forces. Our Indian culture is a good example among all classes of people. The ancient civilisations of India were full-fledged cultures with all modern facilities (for example, the Indus Valley Civilisation, etc.). But with all these, they believed in superstitions. Their religion was mixed up with magical beliefs. They worshiped trees and animals, not because they thought that they were deities but because they firmly believed that they were the dwelling sources for spirits etc., and capable of doing evil or good.

Individuals have to be taught specific religious behavioural patterns such as how to participate in religious activities, how to communicate with a divine being or how to perform prescribed ritual practices and ceremonies. Religious beliefs may also be observed in unconscious manner, through participation in religious groups or sometimes merely by getting associated with individual. Religion is a major aspect of culture. It is important because it codifies and expresses the cultural values of the society as a whole. It is one of the agencies of social control. It also functons for the welfare of human society. A greater part of human life is shaped by religion. It plays a vital and significant role in the life of Indian people. According to Dr. Sarma, it is the sole unifying factor among many diversities of the Indian population (Sarma, T.N., 1980 : 11).

Religion is almost a universal social phenomenon, pervasive in all human societies. It is very essential for human life. It is an institution whose significance cannot be under-valued. It is a source of one's own felicity and peace. It provides immense ethical values and a true meaning to existence. It also gives guidelines for conduct and defines the ends and means in human affairs, human relations and human interactions.

Religion has been defined and interpreted by different scholars in different ways. Tylor (1832—1917) in has book *Religion and cultures An introduction to Anthropology of Religion* defines as "a belief in supernatural being" (Taylor, E.B., 1968 : 49). As has been pointed out by Kroeber, "religion is an important means of socio-cultural change and culture is that complex whole which includes knowledge, beliefs, art, morals, law, customs and any other capabilities acquired by man as a member of society" (Kroeber, A.L., 1948: 212). Change in culture is brought by means of change in system of values. From this definition, one can derive that religion is the best instrument of social change.

Emile Durkheim (1858–1917) observes religion as "a unified system of beliefs and practices related to sacred things—that is to say things set apart and forbidden, beliefs and practices which united into one single community called a Church" (Derkheim, Emile, 1957 : 47)

According to Dr. S. Radhakrishnan, "religion is not the acceptance of academic abstractions or the celebration of ritual ceremonies. It is insight into the nature of reality (*darsana*) or experience of reality (*anubhave*)". (Radhakrishnan, S., 1971: 13). He defines religion as "freedom from fear" (abhaya). Religion is the conquest of fear, the antidote to failure and death (Radhakrishnan, S., 1940 : 44–46). Max Muller states religion as "a struggle to conceive the inconceivable to utter the unutterable a longing of the infinite" (Muller, Max, F, 1972 : 18).

In the words of Swamy Vivekananda, "religion is its own end. That religion which only is a means to worldly well-being is not religion, whatever else it may be. The very end and purpose of all religions is to realise God. Worshipping God is the greatest act. One must bear in mind that religion does not consist in talk, doctrines or books but in realisation, it is not learning but being" (Chidananda Swamy (Ed.), 1964 : 248–50) He affirms that religion is the realisation of God only. He further says that "people must become divine by realising the divine. Idols, temples, churches or books only support or help his spiritual childhood but on and on, he must progress. Man must realise God, feel God, see God and talk of God. That is religion".

The major religious groups in India are Hindus, Muslims, Christians, Sikhs, Jains, Zorastrains (Parsees) and Animatists. Despite the presence of diverse religious groups, India is a secular state. Faith, tolerance, brotherhood and respect for other religions are the main constituents of secularism. The corner stone of all religions is belief in one God (Prabhu, R.K. and U.R. Rao, 1946 : 84). Evils like communalism, fanaticism, casteism and regionalism cannot be removed from Indian society so long as religion is viewed, understood and interpreted in narrower sense.

The Nineteenth century social scientists like H.B. Tylor (1832—1917), Fustel de Coulanges (1830—1889), Robertson Smith (1846—1894) and Emile Durkheim (1858 1917) called the original as 'Primitive religion' mainly based on spiritualism (belief in spiritual beings) and supernaturalism (belief in supreme deity). Whereas, Twentieth century social scientists like Radcliffe Brown (1881—1945), Malinowski (1854—1942), Herbert Spencer (1820—1903) and James George Frazer (1854—1941) viewed the later religion "civilised" or "advanced religion" based on "fetishism' (The worship of inanimate object by savages for its magical powers), Polytheism (the Worship of many Gods) and Monotheism (belief in one God). As the sample in our study constitutes Hindus, Christians and Muslims, it may be good and essential for us to acquaint ourselves with the general tenets contained in each of the three major religions of the world—Hinduism, Islam and Christianity. In the following pages, the tenets and beliefs have been briefly examined and presented.

Hinduism

Many of the Hindu customs and manners are within the rigid framework of orthodoxy and conservatism. The Aryans brought along with them their own beliefs and customs when they migrated. The Vedic Aryans came to adapt themselves with the then prevailing conditions in our country and their customs, beliefs and practices were intermingled with the native one. After the Vedic period the Aryans continued to be steeped in religious beliefs and practices. Then, the religion was purely formal and it became loaded with symbolic subtleties. The atmosphere from the twelfth to the late nineteenth century was surcharged by magical beliefs, spells, rites, ritual practices and numerous deities were chiefly associated with ritual practices. The advent of British and their administration changed the scene to some extent. Western education and ideas lessened the intensity of these beliefs and even brought to light their very irrationality and worthlessness. But beliefs and ritual practices which had from time immemorial been entrenched in the minds of Hindus could not be wiped off and hence in the twentieth century we find various religious beliefs and ritual practices still nourished by them.

Though India is a secular state, Hinduism is the major religion professed by a large number of people. Hinduism is one of the oldest religions in the world. It is not established by any individual. It is a way of life. It is the sum total of various religious experiences and teachings of many sages and saints of ages and ages. It is a growth of ideas, ritual practices and beliefs so comprehensive as to include anything between atheism and pantheism. It is an amalgamation of Indo-Aryan Dravidian and pre-Dravidian religious elements.

The traditional name for Hinduism is Sanatana Dharma" or "Vaidika Dharma" (the eternal dharma). Hindusim is eternal and ageless (sanatana). It has no known founder and is considered to have existed for all time. The word 'Hindu' has its interesting origin. Hindu is a Persian word and it means simply 'Indian'. The Persian invaders could not pronounce 'Sindhu' (the land water by the river Indus) (Batsman, A.L., 1954 : 1). Hence, they called it 'Hindu'. Thus the word "Hindu" emerged from 'Sindhu'. Then the term 'Hindu' was first used by the Mohammadans under foreign domination as unconverted native Indians (Weber, Max, 1967 : 4). For them, the 'Hindu' religion was identified with the Indian people.

Hinduism is the religious expression of the very stuff of Nature and the Divine as the Hindus see them perpetual change seen against a changeless and timeless background. It is also a dharma. It is derived from the root dharma which means 'to hold together'. In this sense, it is 'Law', both the eternal law that governs Nature and the moral law that rules or should rule among men. Hinduism is a polytheistic religion but a polytheism that is also in some sense a monotheism—a principle, i.e., it first regarded as being an impassive absolute but which may also appear as a personal God.

Hinduism is a continuation of the Vedic tradition and it holds the four sacred Vedas, namely *Rigveda, Samaveda, Yajurveda* and *Atharvaveda* and the Vedic pantheon. The Hindus believe religion that the salvation (Moksha) is attained through the paths of action (Karma), of knowledge (Jnana) and of devotion (Bhakti).

According to Karma theory, the Hindus believe in the existence of an entity called 'soul' and re-incarnation of soul (soul in Hinduism called Jeevatma). Hinduism postulates that the soul is liberated from the body with death and the soul thereafter, may for sometime reside in space and/or enjoy heaven or suffer hell before it reincarnates in some form on earth or may not have re-birth at all if its liberation from the body is complete. This eternal release of the soul from the body is called salvation or *moksha* or *mukti* or the union of the soul with God.

Hinduism is a vast subject and an elusive concept. To define it is indeed a difficult and delicate task because it is wide and universal in its scope. Nevertheless an attempt has been made to define it by several scholars.

According to Sen, 'Hinduism' is that which a Hindu does, in other words "it is a question of ritualistic and social observance" (Sen, Guruprasad, 1893 : 9). Buitenen says, "Hinduism is that complex of culture, religious practice, myth, belief that are felt to be continuation of the Vedic tradition" (Buitenen, Van, J.A.B., 1963 : 25).

For practical purposes the explanation given by Lyall may be considered. As he says, "Hinduism is the collection of rites, worships, beliefs, traditions and mythologies that are sanctioned by the sacred books and ordinances of the Brahmans and are propagated by Brahmanic teaching. And a Hindu is one who generally follows the rules of conduct and ceremonies thus laid down for him, particulary regarding food, marriage and the adoration of the Gods" (Lyall, A, 1889 : 114).

According to 1981 Census Report, a little over 453 millions (82.72 per cent) of the total population of 548 millions constitute Hindus. As per the 1991 census, their total population stands at 549, 779, 481. Hindusim being the religion of the majority it provides a basis for national unity. It unites more than two-thirds of the Indian population by means of common deities, common belief systems, common ideals, common scriptures, common ritual practices, common festivals, common worship, common customs etc.

Development of Hinduism

Unlike the other religions of the world, Hinduism has no founder. It is very difficult to trace the historical origion of Hinduism, as a religion. However, it can be known from Vedas. It was during the Fifth and Sixth Centuries B.C. i.e., at the time when the original activity of the Vedic ritual came to an end and the old Vedic framework was lost itself, the tone was set for all the larer development of the highly complex religion.

Historically speaking, Hinduism has its base in the Four Vedas including the Upanishads, the Smrtis or Dharmasastras like those of Manu, Yagnavalkya, Sankhya Likhita, Parasara etc., the Puranas and the Upapuranas, the Itihasas and the Bhagavadgita, the six Vedangas including the Srauta, Grhya, Dharma sutras and the six Hindu philosophical systems (Chatterjee, S.C. 1950 : 2).

The three principle stages or phases in the development of Hinduism are ;

1. Vedism ;
2. Brahmanism and
3. Hinduism.

Vedism

Vedism was the earliest form of the Hindu religion. It is considered to be the most ancient form of Hinduism. Vedism is to be distinguished from Hinduism because the former is characterised by its emphasis on the ritual practices and sacrifices, the latter by devotion to particular deities. Veda means "wisdom" or "Knowledge".

There are four Vedas, the Rig-veda, the Sama-veda, the Yajur-veda and the Atharva-veda The Rig-veda, composed between 1500 and 900 B.C. – i.e., during an interval of 600 years – is the earliest of the Vedas and one of the oldest religious texts in the world still considered sacred. The Sama-veda consists of selected verses from the Rig-veda, to be chanted during rituals by the chanting priest. The Yajurveda is a manual of sacrificial formulas in prose and verse, for the use of the priest who performed the physical operations in the sacri-ices. The Atharva-veda, the fourth of the Vedas, was late in gaining recognition and its status has always been lower than that of the other Vedas. Much of its content is devoted to magical prayers and spells, which point to its derivation from the religion of the common people, both Aryan and non-Aryan.

The Vedic religion constitutes a trinity of deities – the Fire God, the Rain God and the Sun God – one for each of the three worlds – Earth, Air and Sky. Vedic religion primarily consists of sacrifices made to the three Gods in order to appease them. In the Yajurveda one finds that there were two types of sacrifices performed by the Vedic aristocracy. They include soma offerings and animal sacrifices. There were also new-moon and full-moon sacrifices. One finds special ceremonies like Raja Suya Yaga (a king's inauguration ceremony) and the Ashvamedha Yaga (the great horse sacrifice) exclusively performed by kings. The private ritual ceremonies were done by the head of the family.

Brahmanism

The second stage or phase of the Hindu religion was Brahmanism, an out-growth of Vedism. Its development was gradual and extended over many centuries i.e., from eighth century B.C. to twelfth century A.D.

In Vedic times, as has been observed, a perpetual feeling pervaded after one Supreme Being might be found in Air or Sky. So the people turned from polytheism (belief in many Gods) and strove to find out a philosophic basis for the Divine. Brahmanism stressed the Vedas, ritual practices and the hierarchical system of the Hindu society i.e.. caste system. During this period, there began to emerge the doctrines of maya, karma and transmigration of souls which were to become the most characteristic feature of later Hinduism.

Hinduism

Hinduism is the fusion of corrupt Vedic doctrines and non-Aryan aboriginal cults. It contains all religious beliefs and ritual practices of modern India. It is a theistic or monotheistic religion. It is also polytheistic. But polytheism in some sense a monotheism which means that the Gods are only manifestations of an immanent and unitary principle which is the ground of the universe.

In the early years of the Thirteenth Century the Hindus were divided into three sects Saivites, Saktas and Vaishnavites. They were based on the philosophy of supremacy of one God.

The tenets of Hinduism are—

1. The non-duality of the God Head.

2. The divinity of the soul.
3. The unity of existence.
4. The harmony of religions.
5. The theory of Karma and Rebirth.

Caste System

Caste is the structural basis of Hindu society in India. It is a fixed and rigid institution. The caste system is arranged in a hierarchy with the Brahmins at the apex. The social status is ascribed to the individual by his birth in a particular caste group. The Brahmin superiority and established occupational functions of the different castes enabled the Brahmins to take unfair advantages of their unalterable hereditary superior position in society i.e., of scholarly and priest work. Hence, the powerful priestly class emerged in the Hindu social structure. This condition of dominance of priests in society over-emphasised the unexplained religious beliefs and ritual practices. According to the laws of Manu and Vedas there existed four main castes namely Brahmans (Priests or intellectuals), Kshatriya (Warriors and also rulers), Vaisyas (traders and agriculturists) and Sudras (serfs or labourers). In addition to this division, those who did not fall under chaturvarnas were called as outcastes.

Although this general pattern of the four major castes is continuing, there are actually more than four thousand castes in India. Membership in Hindu society is determined by ascribed status that is by birth in a particular caste. Caste regulates ritual practices and belief systems. Each caste is autonomous having its own rules of conduct and customs.

Islam

Islam is one of the old religions of world. It was born in Arabia and founded by Mohammad (571-632 A.D.) in the Seventh Century A.D. The English name for Islam is

"Mohammadanism". The Arabic word 'Islam' means "the act of resignation" or "submission" (Rao, Raja, M.B., 1966, Vol. I: 46).

Mohammad felt revolted by the idolatry and licentiousness of the people around him. He condemned idolatry and started preaching the doctrine of 'one God'. He fled from Mecca to Medina. Thereafter, the believers swelled rapidly and Islam had spread throughout Arabia. The teachings of Mohammad are contained in the Holy Quran which draws largely from Judaism and Christianity with whose theology Islam has much in common.

Muslims use the word 'Allah' for God. Islam postulates only one God, Allah in the place of Polytheism. The way of life of Muslims and their Islamic Institutions have changed from time to time. Muslims accept the absolute word 'God' in the Quran and Prophet's decisions, his precepts, his acts and practices, negative as well as positive.

The Muslims came to South India as traders from Arab lands in Seventh Century and they were welcomed and granted some special facilities by local kings in recognition of their services to the trade. Muslims also came to India in the wake of the military conquests from the North in order to spread Islamic faith. With the advent of invasion of Sind by Muhammad Ibn Kasim in Seventh Century and the establishment of the Delhi Sulthnate in the Thirteenth century, there began a steady flow of Muslim scholars, religious leaders and other professionals, mostly of Turkish, Persian and Afgan origin into India. Islam later split up into two sects, Sunnis and Shias. Sunnis constitute a minority of the Muslim population and are found in Asia, Africa and Europe. The majority of Shias are found in Iran, Iraq and Afghanistan. India has both Shias and Sunnis.

The religious tenets of Islam as mentioned by Siadiqi, Mohammad Mazharuddin in his book : ***What is Islam*** ? are :

1. The conception of God is the basis and foundation of Islam.
2. Belief in survival after death.
3. Belief in the prophets of God.
4. Belief in the books of God.
5. Belief in the Angels of God.
6. No distinction between state and church.
7. Women are inferior to men.
8. Non-belief in racial superiority.

Muslims in India form the second largest population. As per the 1981 Census, a little over 61 millions (61,417,934) constituted Muslims. In 1991 Census, a slight increase has been noticed, i.e., their total population stood at 75,512,439 comprising 11.35 per cent of the total population. Today, India can boast herself of having the second largest Muslim population in the world.

Christianity

Christianity was founded by Jesus Christ in the First Century A.D. Chirstianity as a religion paved the way for social change and progress in India during the British rule.

Christianity is a monotheistic religion. Originally, Christianity has been the most offensive religion of the world, because it preaches the highest doctrines of moral conduct including truth, purity and love to all even to the enemies.

Christianity accepts the dual conception of God and Devil. It also accepts the conceptions of Heaven and Hell, Resurrection and the Day of Judgement and the inspiring Doctrine of Repentance.

According to 1981 Census, the Christians constituted 14 millions (2.60 per cent) of the total population. They are the third biggest community and widely distributed all over India. They are found in the South and especially more in number in the States of Kerala, Nagaland and Mizoram. Their total population as per the 1991 Census was 16,165,447 registering 14 per cent increase over the 1981 Census. Now their percentage of population is 2.43.

The following are the main tenets of Christianity :

1. Love thy neighbour as thyself.
2. Be pure in spirit.
3. Be sorrowful to those who sorrow.
4. Be meek and humble.
5. Be hungry and thirsty for righteousness.
6. Be merciful.
7. Be peace makers.
8. Be pure in heart.
9. Stand firm in the persecution for the sake of righteousness.
10. Take no revenge.
11. Love your enemics.
12. Help the needy ones but without publicity.

All religions, however, have certain common characteristic features regardless of their differences. All religions emphasis the oneness of God. They are based on a particular faith in the existence of reality of fact. This reality or fact may be conceived as a personal God.

Working Women in India

With the advent of British rule in India and the spread of Western education, remarkable changes have taken place in the Hindu Society which affected the status and position of women. The traditional idea of woman's proper place was home has undergone a profound change. An educated working woman seldom feels happy with the exclusively onerous task of bearing and rearing children. She also wants to lead a life of her own outside home like her husband where she can breathe the air of freedom and realise her personal ambitions by pursuing a way of new life. It is quite natural, since a qualified or talented woman cannot rest content with her domestic role of a mother and wife, whose world is totally conditioned by a sense of self-abnegation.

Indian women do not like the idea of taking jobs or continuing with them after marriage. It can easily be accounted as the traditional concept of different roles for both the sexes in our society, deep-rooted and that our inter-relations with the Western countries have not changed our basic attitude very much. The entry of married women into the labour force in India has led to a conflict between the two roles of woman—that of a house wife and that of an earning member. As regards the motivation of work, money is an important factor. The need for extra income for the maintenance of family coupled with the demand for labour from the work sphere is the greatest incentive for the female worker of the present day. Now-a-days most of the educated women do not like to be economic burdens of their families or more bed-fellows to their husbands We are now witnessing a transitional period in the status of women in India. Women are employed both in organised and unorganised sectors as professionals, skilled and unskilled.

Indian women are employed as diplomats, ministers, doctors, vice-chancellors, professors, engineers, lawyers, officers, clerks etc. Women are also found in the fields of police service, military and postal services. All this is due to changes in the traditional system and cultural values of Hindu society. There have been remarkable changes in the status and position of women in India in the last century especially after Independence.

Employment is entirely a new field for women folk. In the olden days it was the monopoly of males. Though the status of woman is considerably improved as compared to the past, it cannot be regarded as being emancipated from the old traditions and customs. Hindus did not favour women taking up jobs of various types. The traditional attitude is still persisting the Indian society. Notwithstanding the traditional idea. women are compelled to go for jobs as there is pressure from family side for financial reasons.

Need And Importance of The Study

With the advent of Independence in India innumerable studies on women have come into existence. The problems, social evils, inequality and discrimination faced by women have drawn a great deal of attention from academicians, social reformers and politicians as well. All these studies have examined and analysed the problems of difficulties faced by woman from different angles. Some are discriptive and some empirical in nature. Many aspects affecting woman's progress and development have been carefully studied and analysed. As a result, there has been a phenomenal increase in the number of studies. Despite all these studies and despite suggestions and recommendations made by the researchers, the status and position of woman has not been improved to the expected level for various reasons. As the root of the problem of woman's poor progress and development lies illiteracy and ignorance. The evil of discrimination against woman begins at birth and continues to persist till she grows, lives and dies.

The numerous studies that appeared in the past three to four decades have thrown light on various social-economic aspects of the problems of women highlighting the factors inhibiting their emancipation and progress. Significant studies on the working women, their plight and their professions, the attitudinal changes as result of taking up employment outside home have also come into limelight. These studies have shown conflicting and interesting findings, many of them however were inconclusive and limited in scop. In spite of them, many more studies are expected to come into existence since women are continually exploited and discriminated. There has been a growing recognition for these studies and it may be interesting to utilise them for proper evaluation and understanding of women's psyche and problems.

In the light of these studies and observations, the present study assumes greater significance and importance. In our study a worthwhile attempt has been made to analyse, examine and assess the changes in the religious attitudes and beliefs and ritual practices of working women in Tirupati. With the background of various studies contributed to women, the present study has been undertaken with the specific aim to examine the working women's religosity, faith and beliefs. It may be said that the studies of this nature will create a proper atmosphere of understanding of the general dynamics of continuity discontinuity and change of the religious attitudes and traditional values which may be of helpful and useful for societal change and development and progress of women.

Statement of the Problem

Society as a whole cannot be understood unless the relationship between various institutions are studied and religion plays an important role in codifying and expressing the cultural values of the divine society. It is viewed that religion cannot be isolated from other social institutions. It has significant influence upon family patterns, economics, politics, technology and other important areas of life. The influence is full and not one-sided. In fact, the secular institutions in turn affect religious forms, values and intensity of beliefs.

Contemporary sociologists and some social anthorpologists are mainly concerned with the study of religious behaviour patterns and ritual practices. Not withstanding the abstract religious principles, the day-to-day religious practices and beliefs system can be understood through the study of rituals. Anthropologists such as Robertson Smith, Franz Boaz, A.R. Radcliffe Brown, E.B. Malinowski, S F. Nadel, Turner and others recognised the importance of various types of ritual practices. A.R. Radcliffe Brown says "...in attempting to understand a religion, it is on the rites rather than on the beliefs that we should first concentrate our attention (Brown, Radcliffe A.R. 1964 : 155).

A rite or ritual is performed with a particular belief, its efficacy is in achieving a certain end or giving certain kind of emotional satisfaction. Whether a rite or ritual is performed due to anxiety as believed by H.B. Malinowski due to expected behaviour pattern is not for us at the moment to indulge in detailed discussion. Following George C. Homans, the Researcher takes a reconciliatory and realistic view that the ritual serves "a function in helping the group to survive both by giving confidence to individual and by solemnising for the group activities of essential importance" (Homans, George, C. 1950 ; 330). It is particularly of interest to note that while periodical rituals in terms of community wide festivals and celebrations mostly reveal the communal impact, the rites such as rites of passage reveal the anxious moments in an individual life and their importance to the family group. Ideally, an account of both the types in different contexts would bring the light, the major characteristics and functions of religious beliefs and ritual practices.

It is held that like any other socio-cultural institutions, religious institutions would also undergo change over a period of time and this change may originate from within or may be due to outside contact. As social situations change so might the religion gets transformed to suit the conditions. Due to voluntary adoption (occasionally sometimes by means of force) certain new beliefs might creep into the system.

OBJECTIVES OF THE STUDY

Based on the need, importance and scope of of the study, the following specific objectives were framed :

1. To find out the religious behaviour patterns and changes both in periodic and non-peridic ritual practices of working women,especially Hindu working women in their day-to-day life.

2. To examine the changes in religious beliefs of the working wemen.

3. To study the sociological determinants such as education and income in governing the changes practising or non-practising the rituals and religious beliefs.

4. To find out whether to what extent the changes have been affected and to what extent such changes would be retained.

Besides these main objectives, the other supplemented objective is to study the socio-economic background of the respondents in general.

Methodology

The present study was conducted in Tirupati town, a well known Hindu pilgrimage centre, in Chittoor district in the State of Andhra Pradesh. Tirupati town is fast developing and increasingly urbanised. It has all the characteristic features of an urban city. Many educational institutions besides three prominent universities namely, Sri Venkatswara Uniuersity, S.P. Mahila Vishwavidyalaya and Sanskrit University are located here. Further, it is growing industrially and commercially. A good number of Government and private organisation offices are concentrated in this town. These offices have many working women. It is for these practical reasons, the town has been chosen for the study. In addition, the author herself is a resident of this town and hence, she could find it easier to collect data from the respondents.

The study was based on 300 working women, selected by using the Randome Sampling method. The sample comprised 27 Hindus (90.3 per cent), 21 : Christians (7.1 per cent) and 8 Muslims (2.6 per cent).

Sample

Religion	*Number of Respondents*	*Percentage*
Hindus	271	90.3
Christians	21	7.1
Muslims	8	2.6
Total	300	100.0

The Hindu respondents included women from different castes broadly categorised into three groups. Backward castes consisting of Brahmin, Kapu, Kamma, Visya, Nair, Balija and Maharastra Brahmin, the Backward castes comprising Vishwan Brahmin, Yadava, Gandla, Besta, Rajaka (Chakali), Dasari, Karanam, Odde, Jangams, Sale, Kummara, Dudekula and the last group included Scheduled Castes (see Table 2).

The respondents possessed different educational qaulifications ranging from primary and secondary education to graduation, post-graduation and professional courses including technical (see Table – 8). The age of the respondents was also taken into account for the proper evaluation and understanding of changes. They were between the ages of 15 and 50 and above (see Table 3).

Necessary data were obtained by means of questionnaire and Participation. An elaborate questionnaire consisting of questions pertaining socio-economic background of the respondents, their beliefs and disbeliefs, performance and non-performance, observing and non-observing of several religious beliefs and ritual practices, was prepared in English and administered to the respondents. Each respondent was met personally and provided with the questionnaire. Sufficient time was given for filling the answers. Later, the filled questionnaires were collected and the information supplied therein was kept confidential in accordance with the wishes of the respondents. They were given full freedom in answering the questions. The data collection was not as tedious as was feared, but in fact turned out to be very interesting and encouraging. The attitude of the respondents was quite positive and they did not hesitate in responding to the author's chief motives in pursuing the subject that was of academic interest and significance. The respondents were quite cooperative and willing to answer the questions. The subject for them was otherwise proved to be rather interesting.

After the field work was over, the collected data was processed and computerised. Necessary tables were drawn. The percentage was calculated by employing simple percentage method. Later, the data was properly analysed and interpreted to draw conclusions.

The material was organised into five chapters. The first chapter is introduction, in which the background of the topic, statement of the problem, need and importance of the study, objectives, methodology and topography of Tirupati town have been presented. Second chapter is devoted to study the socio-economic composition of the respondents. Third chapter examines rites of passage. The religious outlook of the respondents has been dealt within the fourth chapter. Changes in the form of findings and conclusions have been incorporated in fifth chapter.

Topography of Tirupati

Tirupati is one of the most famous places of pilgrimage in India situated almost at the extremity of Andhra Pradesh in the Chittoor district. Tirupati is a Municipal town comprising an area of 1.5 square miles popularly called as a 'Seshachala Hills'. It stands at 13°-41′ North latitude and 79°-24′ east longitude.

Tirupati is included in South Central Railway of India. It is eight miles away from Renigunta, an important railway junction situated on the Madras-Bombay broadguage line. People from all over India have to change the train at Renigunta for Tirupati. However, Tirupati has direct trains to Hyderabad, Bangalore, Vijayawada, Madras, Puri and Calcutta. It has direct road transport facilities connecting important places in South India. Tirupati is also linked by air to Madras, Hyderabad, Bangalore and Vijayawada.

Tirupati is a sacred place for Hindus. It has many temples in and around. Among all the temples, there are three temples namely Sri Rama, Sri Govindaraja Swamy and Sri Varadaraya Swami situated within the town. To the South-East of Tirupati is situated the temple of the consort of the Lord Sri Venkateswara namely Padmavati Devi in Tiruchanur. So also about 11

Kms to the West of Tirupati, we find another temple of Kalyana Venkateswara Mangapuram. The most prominent is the historic shrine of Lord Sri Venkateswara situated on the Tirumala Hills. Tirumala is situated on the hills to the north of Tirupati at a distance of 10 Kms.

The shrine is located atop Tirumala, a cluster of seven hills known as "Seshachalam" with an elevation of 853 metres (3,600 ft.), above the sea level. Special buses are run to the uphills by the Tirumala Tirupati Devasthanams. Many orthodox pilgrims reach the shrine on foot. The Tirumala Tirupati Devasthanams perhaps is the richest religious institution in India. The average annual income of the temple is Thirty six crore rupees. Since 1950, its annual income has been on the increase. It has in recent years launched many educational, cultural and philanthrophic activities. It has established an institution called "Hindu Dharma Prathisthapana" in order to promote and propagate the Hindu Dharma. The temple receives thousands of pilgrims everyday from all parts of India throughout the year. The temple celebrates innumerable festivals, among which the most famous and important is Brahmotsavam which is celebrated for nine days every year in September. This particular festival attracts thousands of pilgrims all over India particularly from the South.

Apart from the religious sanctity attached to the place, Tirupati is the second largest educational centre in Andhra Pradesh. It has three universities, Sri Venkateswara University, Sri Padmavati Women's University and the Sanskrit University, besides professional colleges like engineering, medical, polytechnic, veterinary and agriculture as well as many other degree colleges. Besides, it has developed into an important cultural seat of southern India. Every year Thyagaraja and Annamacharya Cultural Festivals are arranged by the Tirumala Titupati Devasthanams and a large number of scholars and musicians of eminence and reputation are invited to give concerts. Above all, Tirupati is growing as a busy commercial and industrial town. An Industrial Township with an area of 11 Kms has been created between Renigunta and Tirupati. Many small-scale industries have been established in addition to the Railway Workshop which has now come up.

2

Socio-Economic Composition

Understanding of any society or group involves an analysis of the basic elements of its structure and the inter-relationship among these elements. It is recognised that any social organisation in regard to its actual behaviour is strongly influenced by its structural tenets. Socio-Economic background of the respondents is an integral part of any sociological investigation. Hence, this study is all the more important and relevant as it throws light on the socio-economic composition of the respondents.

The status and position of women in any society is an index of the standard of its social organisation. Hinduism has assigned a high place to woman in its religious and social organisations. In the Vedas she is referred as 'the Queen' and 'the Mistress of the household'. A woman performs different social roles as a sister, daughter, wife and mother at different stages in her life. A woman plays a vital role in the life of a man. Woman commands a respectable place in the family, community, society, nation and the world.

According to Lowie (Lowie, R.H. 1960 : 178), the status of woman can be evaluated on the basis of legal status, actual treatment, opportunity for social participation and extent of work.

Though almost all the community in the Hindu society have patrilineal descent and the inheritance of the property through the male lines, the woman certainly has much say in the house and takes decisions on policy matters and plays an important role in all social, economic, political and religious spheres. She has equal rights in selecting her life partner or in certain cases in giving divorce. Yet, sometimes, she may be manhandled by her husband. Generally, a woman who has born children is respected and honoured much more than a barren woman. In the economic activities a working woman does undertake many responsibilities such as working with her husband in the concerned institute or office, in addition to her customary domestic work. In the traditional political structure of the Hindu society, women did not find proper place. After the introduction of Panchayat Raj system in 1960s, women have been actively participating in public activities. Their active participation in the political activities is only a recent change. In spite of their participation in political field one can conclude that in practically every field they enjoy only a moderate freedom in their social status.

Status and Position of Women in India : An Historical Perspective

For the purpose of understanding the changing position of women in India, it is essential for us to acquaint ourselves with the status and position of women in the ancient times, from the Vedic period down to the Nineteenth Century A.D. Hence, a brief survey of the four different periods of the evolution of Indian society is considered and presented in the following pages. The periods are : (i) the age of the Vedas (2500 to 1500 B.C.), (ii) the age of the Brahmanas (1500—500 B.C.), (iii) the age of the Sutras and the Epics (500 B.C. to 500 A.D.).

In Ancient Hindu society women enjoyed equal status as was exercised by men in all aspects. Right from the early Vedic period up to 300 B.C., women were held in high esteem. Women were educated as the boys were and they participated in cultural, social, economic, philosophical and political activities.

The Vedas, the Upanishads and the Puranas contain innumerable schorlars, poets, philosophers and politicians. They used to perform and observe various religious rites, rituals, ceremonies and other festivals. They worshipped various deities by offering various types of food. A man and a woman had complete equality in performing religious duties. Women were treated with great respect both within and outside the home. They were treated as the embodiment of the Goddess of wealth, strength and wisdom (Lakshmi, Sakti and Saraswati). In this connection, Manu said that where women were neglected all rites and ceremonies were fruitless and that family quickly perished but where women did not grieve it prospered (Motwani, K., 1958 : 110). The birth of a female child was equally welcomed, they were educated as the boys were, and their education was considered so important that the Atharva Veda asserted that the success of woman in her married life depends upon her training during Brahmacharya period of celibacy and student life, for which both boys and girls were initiated alike.

Women took part in public life and also entered the teaching profession. The age at marriage of girls was between 16 and 17 years. Being educated and grown-up, they had a voice in mate-selection. Martrimony was not compulsory for a woman, and no limitation was placed on her age at marriage.

In the eyes of religion, a man and a woman had complete equality. The wife was an absolute necessity in religious services, and this circumstance helped to raise her status. In the home her position was an honoured one, and monogamy was the rule. Widow remarriage was allowed, though it took place usually within the family with the younger brother of the deceased husband. Divorce was permitted. In the *Rig-Veda* one finds no reference to the practice of Sati—the burning of widows with their dead husband. It has been established beyond doubt through literary and historical research the women held a position of equality with man during the Vedic period.

During the age of the Brahmanas (1500 B.C. – 500 B.C.), though changes in the position of woman had started taking place, these were very gradual and, by and large, woman enjoyed the same rights and privileges and occupied an honoured position in the home. She could move about freely both within and outside the home and take useful part in public affairs.

It was during the age of the Sutras and the Epics (500 B.C to 500 A.D.) that the position of women started deteriorating considerably. The birth of a daughter was considered ominous in the family, whereas the son was a source of happiness and rejoicing. The Aitereya Brahmana says "a daughter is a source of misery and that a son is the saviour of the family" (Apte, V.M., 1954 : 18). Child marriages increased. Widow remarriage was opposed and prohibited. Daughters could not be given complete instruction in Vedic studies. Sons alone could discharge certain ritual obligations to ancestors, and thus became a religious necessity derived and valued much more than daughters. Women were deprived of all their fundamental rights, justice, freedom, education and equality.

A few factors have been found to be responsible for the lowering of their position after 300 B.C. One of them was that since the Aryans had to encounter various tribal people inhabiting the Gangetic plains, sons were valued more because they could help them in the wars against these people. Another reason put forth is that rituals connected with Vedic sacrifices became more complicated and were given more importance. And since, for carrying out Vedic sacrifices, education was needed upto the age of 23 or 24 years, daughters could not be given complete instruction in Vedic studies.

As such, sons alone could discharge certain ritual obligations to ancestors and thus became a religious necessity desired and valued much more than daughters. Yet, another reason advanced by scholars in the introduction of the non-Aryan wife into the household, who with her ignorance of the Hindu religion and Sanskrit language, was declared unfit for religious rituals and thus could not enjoy religious privileges. Gradually, all women were declared unfit for Vedic studies and religious rites. As a consequence of these reasons, woman's education was discontinued, which in turn lowered her age at marriage and also her religious and social status in the home. Whatever the reasons might be, the great changes that had taken place after 300 B.C. led to the lowering of woman's position in the home.

Due to various political conditions and foreign invasions by 700 A.D., the practice of Sati, the spread of purdah, prohibition of widow remarriage and the theory of the perpetual tutelage of women organised by Manu—the supreme law-giver of Hindu society became prevalent. Thus, by 700 A.D., the position of women had considerably deteriorated. It continued to be degraded till 1800 A.D. She was virtually considered a non-entity – a slave or chattel. She had almost no status in society and none in her own estimation. Thus, lack of education, child marriages, polygamy, seclusion, purdah and the practice of Sati brought about a tremendous deterioration in her position at home and in society in general.

Status and Position of Women in Modern Hindu Society

About a century ago, the status and position of women in India was almost the same as it was in the Medieval period. It was only in the Nineteenth Century various socio-cultural and politico-economic circumstances, foreign missionaries, Indian social reformers like Raja Ram Mohan Roy, Iswar Chandra Vidya Sagar, Swami Vivekananda, Mahadeo Govind Ranade and the social, religious and political organisations like the Arya Samaj, the Indian National Congress, the Rama Krishna Mission, the strong women's movements which spearheaded the struggle against the irrational orthodoxy and descrimination and finally Mahatma Gandhi and the Indian National movement brought about significant changes in the existing social pattern through educational, economic and legislative measures. With social reform movements, political progress, cultural renaissance and economic development, the emancipation of women has considerably increased in Hindu society.

Thus, through the efforts of foreign missionaries, social reformers, enlightened women and social legislations during the British period, more rights and privileges were gradually granted to women in India. It was after Independence, women in India have been legally and politically emancipated from their tradition-bound ethos by the virtue of various acts and statutes such as Hindu Succession Act 1956, Hindu Marriage Act 1955, the Hindu Women's Right to Property Act 1937 and the Hindu Law of Inheritance (amendment) Act 1929.

In today's India women has an equal right to education, employment, franchise, inheritance, property, marriage at a mature age, divorce and remarriage as a divorcee or widow in addition to the right of being her husband's only legal wife at a given time. Theoretically, the equality of women has been established. All these increased opportunities of education and employment have brought changes in her position in the home and in society. One finds that more and more women are educated, gaining economic independence and holding official positions and ranks at all levels. They have membership in Indian Parliament, State Assemblies and Local Bodies, and an increasing number are taking an active part in the affairs of the country. The number of widows and divorced re-marrying have increased even among those sections of society which did not allow this at all. No doubt, the traditional conceptions regarding the position of women in India have changed and are still changing.

It is in this context, the changes in family and education and how these changes have affected the status of women in our study have been examined and presented in the following sections..

Status of Working Women in the Family

Today, we are witnessing a transitional period in the status of women in India. Nevertheless, women are holding sub-ordinate position in the family. Seniority in age or in generational status may give a women a higher symbolic rank in relation to certain men in the family, but generally male superiority in the Hindu family is supported by tradition and man's rights of property (Gore, M.S. 1968 ; 156).

The study reveals that a working woman is more systematic and regular in duty as well as in household functions than a man. In fact, a woman's role in the family is far more important than her role outside. Her first duty is towards her home, her husband and her children. A woman's pride is her home. Even the woman in affluent society has to look after domestic chores.

Table 1

Status of Women in the Family

Status of women in the family	*Number of working women*	*Rank*	*percentage*
Equal to men	270	1	90.0
Superior to man	—	—	—
Inferior to men	30	2	10.0
Total	300		100.0

According to the Table 1, 270 respondents (50 per cent) considered themselves equal to men, whereas 30 respondents (10 per cent) inferior to men having the second position. This shows that the position of women as conceived by women themselves is equal to men.

Caste-wise Distribution of the Respondents

The structural basis of Hindu society is caste. Caste embraces not only a very great majority of the population of India, but it forms the normal framework of society and is intimately connected with its religious life too. It has been found possible, therefore, not without apparent justification to regard it as a very soul of this somewhat intermediate, fluid collection of customs and beliefs which is called 'Hinduism'.

In our study, apart from the Christian and Muslim respondents, the Hindu respondents comprising 271 belonged to different castes. Caste-wise distribution of working women is presented in Table 2.

Table 2

Number of Working Women in Different Castes

Castes	*Number of Working women*	*Percentages*
Hindus		
Forward castes :		
Kapu	47	17.34
Kamma	27	9.96
Brahmin	63	23.24
Kshatriya	14	5.16
Balija	34	12.54
Naidu	12	4.42
Nair	2	0.7
Vysya	10	3.69
Maharashtra Brahmin	1	0.36
Backward castes :		
Viswa Brahmin	4	1.47
Yadava	10	3.69
Gandla	16	5.90
Bestha	7	2.58
Rajaka (Chakali)	5	1.84
Kummara	3	1.10
Dudekula	1	0.36
Sale (Devangana)	1	0.36

(*Contd.*)

Dasari	1	0.36
Karanam	4	1.47
Jangam	2	0.7
Scheduled Castes :		
Harijans	7	2.58
Total	271	
Muslims	8	2.6
Christians	21	7.0
Total	29	
Grand Total	300	100.0

Table 2 reveals that out of 300 respondents, 217 belonged to twenty one castes in Hinduism. These castes were categorised into three broad groups : Forward castes, Backward castes and Scheduled ,castes. Of the 271 Hindu respondents, 77.41 per cent represented Forward castes and 20 per cent Backward castes. An insignificant percentage (2.58 per cent) of Hindu respondents belonged to Scheduled Castes. There were no Scheduled Tribe working women. On further analysis, it is found that among the Forward castes, 23.24 per cent belonged to Brahmin community, 17.3 per cent Kapu community and 9.96 per cent Kamma community. The other respondents representing different castes in order were Balija (12.54 per cent) Naidu (4.42 per cent), Vysya (3.69 per cent), Nair (0.7 per cent) Maharashtra Brahmin (0.36 per cent). These castes are forward and advanced in terms of social and economic status.

Age of the Respondents

Age variable has been taken to assess the changes in the religious attitudes of the respondents. Biologically, age signifies the physical and mental maturity of an individual. It has significance in respect of observing or not observing certain religious beliefs and practices. The more one is aged the more one moves towards religion and the more one becomes piety in behaviour. Hence, age has been in the study treated as a crucial detetminant of the respondents' attitudes.

The age variations of the respondents are given in Table 3.

Table 3

Age Groups of the Respondants

Age	*Number of working women*	*Percentages*
15–20	1	0.3
21—30	125	41.7
31—40	107	35.7
41—50	38	12.7
51 and above	29	9.6
Total	300	100.0

The age of the respondents, for the sake of convenience, was divided into five groups. It is discovered that the respondents belonged to different age groups. The data shows that a high percentage of the respondents, that is, 77.4 per cent were found between 21 and 40 years. This means that majority of the respondents were young. Only, 12.7 per cent of the respondents were middle-aged (41-50 years). There were only 20 respondents (9.6 per cent) whose age was found above 51 years. Only one respondent (0.3 per cent) belonged to 15-20 years.

Caste-wise Age Distribution of the Respondents

Caste-wise age distribution of the respondents is illustrated in Table 4.

Caste-wise, it is found that majority of the respondents belonging to 15 Forward castes were seen between 21 and 40

Table 4
Caste-Wise Age Groups of the Respondents

Castes	*15-20*	*21-30*	*31-40*	*41-50*	*51 & above*	*Total*
1	*2*	*3*	*4*	*5*	*6*	*7*
Forward Castes :						
Kapu	1 (2.1)	25 (53.2)	17 (36.2)	3 (6.4)	1 (2.1)	47
Kamma	—	12 (44.4)	10 (37.0)	4 (14.8)	1 (3.7)	27
Brahmin	—	22 (34.9)	22 (34.9)	12 (19.1)	7 (11.1)	63
Kshatriya	—	7 (50.0)	5 (35.7)	1 (7.1)	1 (7.1)	14
Balija	—	13 (38.2)	20 (58.8)	1 (2.9)	—	34
Naidu	—	6 (50.0)	3 (25.0)	3 (25.0)	—	12
Nair	—	2 (100.0)	—	—	—	2
Vysya	—	4 (40.0)	3 (30,0)	1 (10.0)	2 (20.0)	10

1	2	3	4	5	6	7
Maharashtra Brahmin	—	—	—	1 (100.0)	—	1
Backward Castes :						
Viswa Brahmin	—	2 (50.0)	1 (25.0)	1 (25.0)	—	4
Yadava	—	2 (20.0)	4 (40.0)	1 (10.0)	3 (30.0)	10
Gandla	—	9 (56.3)	3 (18.8)	—	4 (25.0)	16
Bestha	—	1 (14.3)	2 (28.6)	2 (28.6)	2 (28.6)	7
Rajaka (Chakali)	—	—	1 (20.0)	2 (40.0)	2 (40.0)	7
Kummara	—	3 (100.0)	—	—	—	3
Dudekula	—	1 (100.0)	—	—	—	1

(Contd.)

1	2	3	4	5	6	7
Sale (Devangana)	—	1	—	—	—	1
		(100.0)				
Dasari	—	—	1	—	—	1
			(100.0)			
Karanam	—	1	1	1	1	4
		(25.0)	(25.0)	(25.0)	(25.0)	
Jangam	—	—	—	2	—	2
				(100.0)		
Scheduled Castes :						
Harijans	—	2	1	1	3	7
		(14.3)	(28.6)	(14.3)	(42.9)	
Total	1	112	95	36	27	271
	(0.4)	(41.3)	(35.1)	(13.3)	(10.0)	
Muslims	—	3	3	1	1	8
		(37.5)	(37.5)	(12.5)	(12.5)	
Christians	—	10	9	1	1	21
Total	—	13	12	2	2	29
		(44.8)	(41.9)	(6.9)	(6.9)	

Grand total : 300

years. It was more or less the same in the case of Backward castes. Interestingly, among Forward castes, respondents belonging to Kapu community were found in all age-groups. Except Kapu community, no other castes were seen in the age group of 15—20 years. The same trend could be seen in the case of Christian and Muslim respondents. Among them, majority of them belonged to 21 and 40 years.

Rural and Urban Background

Rural and urban background of the respondents also affects and shapes the respondents' life styles and attitudes. However, this component has not been taken seriously in our study as all the respondents were found employed in different offices within the town (Tirupati). For understanding purpose, the rural and urban background of the respondents has been assessed. It is evident from our study that 80.3 per cent of the respondents possessed urban background and only 19.7 per cent rural background (see Table 5). The respondents with urban background belonged to Tirupati town itself.

Table 5

Rural and Urban Background of the Respondents

Religion	*Rural*	*Urban*	*Total*
Hindus	51 (18.81%)	220 (81.18%)	271
Christians	8 (38.09%)	13 (61.90%)	21
Muslims	—	8 (100.0%)	8
Total	59 (19.7%)	241 (80.3%)	300 (100%)

Family

Any social institution is relatively enduring configuration of prescriptions, beliefs and practices that are regarded as being essential for the maintenance of society, its structure and its basic values. In India, family is one of the most fundamental social institutions. The traditional Indian social institutions had a powerful hold on all individuals, perhaps it is this factor which has contributed to the preservation of various beliefs in spite of various changes.

Hence, family is the basic unit of social living and action. Family, as an institution, is to be found even in the most primitive of human societies in the world. According to Burgess and Locke (1954 : 26 27), historically the family has undergone several changes from a hard and fast social structure or institution to one that is becoming a flexible human relationship.

Burgess and Locke have defined family as "a group of persons, united by ties of marriage, blood or adoption, constituting a single household interacting and communicating with each other in respective social roles of husband and wife, mother and father, son and daughter, brother and sister and creating and maintaining a common culture" (1954 : 8).

Bernard, F. (1966 : 8), states family as "a collective enterprise based on relationship defined by birth and marriage, in other words, family is essentially a kinship organisation mobilised to endure", MacIver, R.M. (1945 : 230) defines family as "a group defined by a sex relationship sufficiently precise and enduring to provide for the procreation and upbringing of children".

The family in its earliest origins began as a reproductive or biological association, but gradually it has developed into a primary social unit of the highest importance to the individual and the society. The family as an institution has many important functions to perform. It has emerged in order to satisfy certain very basic biological, psychological and social needs of man. And even though recent social and economic changes have deeply affected the form and character of the family, they have not changed the basic biological facts and the social needs which create the essential functions of family. In the words of MacIver, the primary functions of the modern family include the procreation and the care and nurture of the young, the more stable satisfaction of the sex needs of the partners and the sharing of a home, with its combination of material, cultural and affectional satisfactions. In Hindu society, a family performs certain vital functions at four different stages of life.

At the first stage of childhood, a child is looked after by its parents till it attains majority. In the second stage, children obtain adulthood and begin to participate in all socio-economic, religious activities of the family as full-fledged members. At the third stage the individual as a married person assumes a responsible role looking after wife or husband and children. At the final stage as the person becomes old, he/she is taken care of by sons. Generally, the Hindus have patrilineal descent, patrilocal residence and patriprotestale authority.

Family is considered unique in Indian society. The structure of family may be analysed under three broad categories – Joint Family, Extended Family and Nuclear Family. The study is devoted to examine these types of family which exist among working women. It is discovered that an overwhelming majority of the respondents (67.7 per cent) belonged to Nuclear Families.

Joint Family

The joint family in Hindu society, has since long played an important role in preserving and conveying the traditional beliefs and practices. The elders bring up the children in such a manner that they strictly adhere to the beliefs and practices. If any person in the joint family dares to do anything contrary to the accepted pattern of the society in which he lives he or she has to pass through a profound emotional experience.

The ideal model of family system in India since the earliest times has been the Joint Family which incorporates a man and wife, their unmarried daughters and sons and their spouses and their children. Other kin group members are allowed to live together in the joint family. According to Karve, I. (1965 : 8), "joint family is a group of people who generally live under one roof, who eat food cooked at one hearth, who hold property in common and who participate in common worship and are related to each other as some particular type of kindred". It is a self-sufficient unit socially, economically and culturally. The father is the head of the joint family and his sons are supposed to live jointly with their spouses.

Since the turn of the century a number of studies have been conducted to examine the changes in the joint family system. Today radical changes are taking place in the spheres of civic, social, economic and cultural life, which are affecting the patterns of family living. In the words of Dr. A.R. Desai, (1961 : 48), the traditional joint family and the familistic rural framework have been undergoing a qualitative transformation. The basis of rural family relationships is shifting from that of status to that of contract...The family is being transformed from a unit of production to a unit of consumption. The cementing bond of the family is being changed from consanguinity to conjugality". Mehta, in his thought-provoking article "Is the Joint Family Breakingup ?" (*Illustrated weekly of India*, XCIV, September 23), observes that "the joint family in India today is a dying institution. It has lost its validity and is even though to be anti-progressive and therefore anti-modern". The spread of liberal education, the new ideas of equality and self-respect, the value attached to the development of individual personality and the desire for economic and social freedom are some of the main factors which are affecing the pattern of marriage and family life.

Various dimensions of modernisation such as rapid industrialisation, increased urbanisation, higher education, adoption of a democratic value system, introduction of monetary economy and changing occupational structures are held accountable for the break-up of the joint family system being replaced by the nuclear family.

Nuclear Family

The term "nuclear family" (or 'elementary' or 'simple' or 'basic') is most frequently used to refer to a group consisting of a husband, wife and their socially recognised children. It is a universal human social grouping. The nuclear family as a basic unit is present in almost all societies. It is more mobile than the joint or extended families.

Murdock, (1949 : 3) says that the nuclear family is the universal form of family relations, always fulfilling "distinctive and vital functions - sexual, economic, reproductive and educational . . . " The nuclear family has developed as a consequence of the growth of individualism, reflected in property rights, law and general social ideas of individual happiness and self-fulfilment, and as a corollary of geographical social mobility.

Extended Family

An extended family consists of a nuclear family and one or more members other than the parents and married sons. Sometimes, an extended family is connected by having several elementary families under the authority of a parent, uncle or other consanguineal relative. In the following Table 6, the types of families that exist among the working women is presented.

Table 6

Number of Working Women in Joint, Nuclear and Extended Families

Type of family	*Number of Working Women*	*Percentage*
Joint family	15	5.0
Nuclear family	203	67.7
Extended family	82	27.3
Total	300	100.0

The data indicates that an overwhelming majority of the respondents have nuclear families. Their total percentage is 67.7. 27.3 per cent of the respondents have extended families. An insignificant percentage (5 per cent) belong to joint families. This shows the decline and the unpopularity of joint family among the working women. However, it is found that the extended family exists among the working women, though with less popularity and significance. Even this type of family is also on the decline. Nuclear family alone has been accepted as the best and most acceptable form of family unit. The joint family system, the traditional form of family, has completely been broken and has yielded room to nuclear family.

Interestingly, in the data it has been found that the nuclear family was popular among Christians and Muslims. Both these communities have accepted the small family norm for various individual and economic reasons.

A number of factors may be cited for the disintegration of joint fami y. Education has brought a tremendous change in Hindu family structure. To education, we may add the factor of work outside the family which has also yielded to nuclear family. Further, urbanisation has driven a number of women leaving the joint family. Since all the respondents were taken from Tirupati town, its rapid urbanisation and modernisation have effected the family structure.

Attitudes Towards Nuclear Family

When asked what their attitude was towards nuclear family, a greater percentage of the respondents, that is 80 per cent, responded positively. While 20 per cent of the respondents did not favour it. They expressed the desire to remain in joint and extended families.

Table 7

Respondents' Attitude Towards Nuclear Family

Attitude	*Number of respondents*	*Percentage*
Negative	60	20.0
Positive	240	80.0
Total	300	100.0

Significantly as many as 37 respondents in the extended family favoured Nuclear family. For personal reasons they could not come out and lead independent life. However, the respondents in joint family did not favour Nuclear type of family. They were completely satisfied to be one among the larger family members. They had no plans, as expressed by them, to move out and establish independent private life.

In the study it is also found that as many as 82 respondents had extended families, the problem has risen in the case of distinguishing between joint family and extended family. To a question, "are you a member of joint family ?" the respondents who were staying with the father-in-law or mother-in-law, or both, and/or with brothers-in-law and sisters-in-law (husband's sister and/or husband's brother's wife) with their children answered with uncertainity not specifying the exact relation. Notwithstanding this difficulty, the author has viewed such relation as brought under the group of extended family in sociological terminology.

It may be said that the extended family did not bear the onslaughts of modernisation, urbanisation and ideas of individualism. Not only these factors, but also women's education and their setting out for work regularly have not much affected this institution. Also the customary staying and living of parents with their daughters and sons after their marriage has not been broken completely. The presence of at least one elderly family member in the home makes the earning mother more carefree. At least, the old people are neglected. The warmth of human relationship still persists. The daughters feel happier and comfortable to live with their mothers and fathers.

Taking the review of the structure of family in the study, it may be summed up that this basis human institution has undergone significant changes, yielding to the adoption of nuclear family norm due to the influence of modern forces such as modernisation, urbanisation, education and occupational patterns.

Education

Education is an effective social instrument of change. It is social phenomenon. The level of education is an important indication for understading of the present and future status of women in a country. Every dynamic society striving for balanced development attaches great importance to education. During the Vedic period, women were given equal education with men. But, during the time of Muslim rule women had very little opportunities for their education. The life of women became more circumscribed and they had to observe purdah. After independence due importance was given to women's education.

The Government of India as well as the State Government contributed a lot to the fast development of women's education. For example, the Government of India appointed a National Committee for women's Education under the Chairpersonship of Smt. Durgabai Deshmukh. The Committee made certain suggestions which were later carried on. Then in 1959, a National Council for the Education of Women was set up. Most of the State Governments have established State Councils for women's education. A number of States have appointed women as the Deputy Directors of Education in charge of the Departments of Girls' Education. The Central Social Welfare Board has also contributed to the adult women's education. In short, the neglected aspect of education i.e., women's education is now no longer neglected. With the result women's education is flourishing fast. According to Professor Kapadia, "education for women brought about a trenmendous changes in Hindu marriage and in family ideals and practices" (Kapadia, K.M. 1958, 253).

The following Table 8 shows the number of working women in different levels of education.

The data points out that there were no illiterates among working women. All the resondents were educated. They had different levels of education. As per the figures, out of 300 respondents, a little over fifty per cent (that is 51.3 per cent) were post-graduates. Followed by 21.7 per cent were graduates, professionals constituted 8.3 per cent. While 7.3 per cent of the respondents possessed Intermediate qualifications and 7.7 per cent Secondary education. An insignificant percentage, that is 3.60 per cent, had Primary education. On further computation of data, it is learnt that an overwhelming majority of the resondents (81.3 per cent) had higher qualifications, that is, graduation and above graduation. Only 18.60 per cent had school and Intermediate education. All this indicates the progress made by women in the field of education. Women had access to higher education. Even technical and other professional courses were not barred for women.

Table 8

Number of Working Women in Different Levels of Education

Level of education	*Number of Working women*	*Percentages*
Primary education	11	3.60
Secondary education	23	7.7
Matric/Intermediate	22	7.3
Graduation	65	21.7
Post-graduation	154	51.3
Technical	7	2.3
Professional	18	6 0
Total	300	100.0

Education—Caste-Wise Distribution

Caste-wise educational level of the respondents is illustrated in Table-9. The data shows that more than the Backward castes, the Forward caste Hindu working women had higher educational qualification. Among them, respondents

Table 9

Caste-Wise Educational Level of the Respondents

Caste	*Primary education*	*Secondary education*	*Matric/ Inter*	*Gradua-tion*	*Post-Gradua-tion*	*Technical*	*Profe-ssional*	*Total*
1	*2*	*3*	*4*	*5*	*6*	*7*	*8*	*9*
Forward Castes :								
Kapu	03 (06.4)	02 (04.3)	01 (02.1)	08 (17.0)	32 (68.1)	—	01 (02.1)	47
Kamma	—	02 (07.4)	05 (18.5)	09 (33.3)	10 (37.0)	—	01 (03.5)	27
Brahmin	—	03 (04.8)	06 (09.5)	15 (23.8)	36 (57.1)	01 (01.6)	02 (03.2)	63
Kshatriya	—	01 (07.1)	—	03 (21.4)	08 (57.1)	02 (14.3)	—	14
Balija	02 (05.9)	06 (17.7)	01 (02.9)	08 (23.5)	14 (41.2)	—	03 (08.8)	34
Nadiu	—	01 (08.3)	—	02 (16.7)	05 (41.7)	01 (08.3)	03 (25.0)	12

Nair	—	—	—	—	02 (100.0)	—	—	02.
Vysya	—	—	—	02 (20.2)	05 (50.0)	—	03 (30.0)	10
Maharashtra Brahmin	—	—	—	—	01 (100.0)	—	—	01
Backward Castes :								
Viswa Brahmin	—	—	02 (50.0)	01 (25.0)	01 (25.0)	—	—	04
Yadaya	01 (10.0)	01 (10.0)	01 (10.0)	—	04 (40.0)	—	03 (30.0)	10
Gandla	—	01 (06.3)	02 (12.5)	01 (06.3)	10 (62.5)	—	02 (12.5)	16
Bestha	01 (14.3)	—	—	01 (14.3)	04 (57.1)	01 (14.3)	—	07
Rajaka	—	01 (20.0)	—	02 (40.0)	02 (40.0)	—	—	05

(*Contd.*)

Table 9 (*Contd.*)

1	*2*	*3*	*4*	*5*	*6*	*7*	*8*	*9*
Kummara	—	—	—	01 (33.3)	02 (66.7)	—	—	03
Dudekula	—	—	—	—	—	01 (100.0)	—	01
Sale (Devangana)	—	—	—	—	01 (100.0)	—	—	01
Dasari	—	—	—	—	01 (100.0)	—	—	01
Karanam	—	01 (25.0)	01 (25.0)	01 (25.0)	01 (25.0)	—	—	04
Jangam	—	—	—	01 (50.0)	01 (50.0)	—	—	02
Scheduled Castes/ Tribes :								
Harijans	03 (42.9)	—	—	03 (42.9)	01 (14.3)	—	—	07

Total	10 (03.7)	19 (07.0)	19 (07.0)	58 (21.4)	141 (52.4)	06 (02.2)	18 (06.6)	271
Muslims	—	01 (12.5)	02 (25.0)	02 (25.0)	03 (37.5)	—	—	08
Christians	01 (04.8)	03 (14.3)	01 (04.2)	05 (23.8)	10 (47.6)	01 (04.8)	—	21
Total	01 (03.5)	04 (13.8)	03 (12.8)	07 (24.1)	13 (44.8)	01 (03.5)	—	29
Grand total=300								

belonging to Kapu community had higher educational qualifications. That is 68.1 per cent of Kapu respondents possessed post-graduate qualification. Whereas 57.1 per cent and an equal percentage of respondents among Brahmin and Kshatriya communities had post-graduate qualifications. So, it may be seen that among the Forward caste Hindu working women, Kapus, Brahmins and Kshatriyas had higher level of education. They were followed by other caste respondents in descending order: Vysyas, Balijas and Naidus. In the case of Backward caste Hindu working women, majority of them were graduates and post-graduates. Of the seven Harijan respondents, 3 (42.9 per cent) were graduates and only one had post-graduate qualification.

Regarding Muslim and Christian working women, ten Christian respondents (47.6 per cent) and three Muslim respondents (37.5 per cent) possessed post-graduate qualifications. The educational level was high among the respondents of these two communities.

Economic Composition

One of the most important factors which determine the social status of any individual or group of individuals relates to the economic conditions. Every known economic system has been utilising and presumably requiring the work of women and they have been working in practically every such system both for their maintenance and for their satisfaction, as human beings and as members of human society. "With the evolution of an agricultural economy the women's role became more real and defined .. their functions, if different from those of their husbands, were not less important" (Sills, David, L (Ed), 1968 : 442).

Traditionally, woman was expected to work at home and help her husband. But, there is a shift in the structure of work since the industrial revolution and hence, the concept of work has changed. India is primarily an agricultural country and women working outside their homes is not a new phenomenon as they have been always working in agricultural fields by the side of their husbands. The women from the economically least privilaged strata of society have also been working since long for wages in factories as menial servants and as unskilled labourers. It is the urban women of middle and upper classes, specially the married and unmarried women, whose taking up of gainful employment is comparatively a recent phenomenon.

Hobhouse rightly points out that "the education of women and their position in society are a sure index of the advancement of society" (Hobhouse, L.T., 1951 : 65). The taking up of gainful employment by educated middle class women has significant implications for social change. Gustav Geiger, the Swedish Sociologist writes that "the position of women in a society provides an exact measure of the development of that society" (Sullerot, Evenlyne, 1971 : 14). Some of the important and closely integrated components of women's position are ideology, role in the family, role in society, economic role, sphere of activity and sphere of forbidden activity etc. The study of a woman's economic role as well as of her position as a worker would definitely throw light on her position or status in society.

Ward points out in her studies that women workers in India come either from very poor or from very rich strata of society. According to her observations, the very poor work to meet the gross economic necessity, whereas the very rich work to satisfy their intellectual hunger and for self-fulfilment (Barbara), Ward, 1972 : 61). But this is not the situation today. The number of middle class women workers has increased tremendously in the last three decades or so. Before World War II and even till a little later the women from middle and upper classes were mostly confined to their homes. It was considered derogatory for a girl, more so for a married woman, to come out of her home and to take up employment. It is heartening to notice after Independence, women have made a considerable development and progress in taking up employment. They are now occupying various positions in all spheres. In free India, women, both married and unmarried, have been taking up various jobs in increasing numbers.

Among the various environmental and institutional factors contributing to rise in the social position of women in India, the most important have been advances in science and technology and education, national awareness (awareness of one's role in contributing to the nation) and the changes made in law. Consequently, new social roles started emerging both for men and women. Advances in science and technology led to new production processes, occupations and skills, which, in turn, led to an increased demand for women labour. Again, women today enjoy better health because of the progress in the national health programmes including family planning.

As a result, not only are they relieved of their worries and their pre-occupations with matters such as too frequent births and health problems of large families but they can also now afford to invest part of their energies for activities outside their homes. The shift from rural to urban living has also affected changes in the social role of women. The spread of education has also contributed to their seeking of gainful employment in various fields. Not only have many women attained relief from the dawn to dusk toil in village life but they have also gained access to increased employment opportunities vis-a-vis their higher education.

The organised sector in the Indian economy comprises all public sector establishments i.e., all services under central, state and local governments and public sectors mainly industries, banks and public utilities and non-agricultural private sector establishments which employ ten or more persons. It includes all joint stock companies in the private sector which may be grouped as corporate sector. Employment in the organised sector requires certain minimum educational qualifications.

That many more educated women willing to take white collar jobs is evident from the fact that in 1966, 15 per cent of those registered at Indian Employment Exchanges for white collar jobs were women (Report of Planning Commission, 1966), whereas out of those actually employed in these jobs, only 2 to 3 per cent were women. The increasing participation of women in the economic activity in India is reflected by the growth in the number of women employees. The 1961 Census reveals that roughly 28 out of every hundred females were in the labour force. These constituted 52 per cent of the women in the age group 15-59 years, as against 41 per cent in the year 1951.

According to 1971 Census, there were 31 million women workers in India, 28 million in rural areas and 3 million in urban areas. Among the total main workers in 1981 census, 14 per cent were females, of them 16 per cent were found in rural areas and 7.28 per cent in urban areas. Whereas in 1991 census, a slight increase in their percentage of representation against the total Main workers may be noticed. That is, 16.43 per cent of the total Main workers were females. Of these female workers, 19.07 per cent belong to rural areas and 8.62 per cent urban areas. Education and employment of women are very important for national development. The Government is providing several new economic opportunities to the working women to improve their social conditions. Today, women have access to several types of occupations. Equality of opportunities in public employment and office under the state is guaranteed by Article 16. This clause has helped to ensure a significant position and status to Indian working women in various public services. In the unorganised sector the vast majority of women have been employed in agricultural occupations. In the organised sector, majority of women have been employed in the professional, technical and related jobs. We find women being employed as doctors, engineers, administrators and bankers. Besides, they are participating in public activities in large numbers and their role cannot be ignored and undermined.

Two interesting trends are noticeable in the employment pattern of women today. First, in addition to the women from the lower socio-economic strata, women from the middle and upper classes have also started joining the work force. Second, in terms of occupational distribution, a majority of women in India are still employed in traditional occupations, though one could find Indian women employed as executives, administrators, doctors, lecturers, research workers, office workers, etc. Until education is given a vocational bias, it is viewed that a number of educated women will remain unemployed even though they are eager to work. Literacy, education and employment are connected links in the process of social development and have a strong bearing on the status of an individual in the family as well as in the society. Hence, to enhance the status of women, their education and training to equip them for jobs and vocations is vitally important. Their participation in various economic activities is imperative for the development of entire India.

In this context, an attempt has been made in the following pages to examine the economic position of working women in our study. While evaluating and assessing their economic status, an extra care has been taken to avoid any complications and pitfalls. For instance, while assessing the income of the respondents, their income alone was taken into account and not their husbands' income. Further, their income on property was excluded from the calculation. Similarly, while examining savings their individual savings with the exclusion of the family's were considered.

The occupations and functions of the different castes are not wholly exclusive but the economic system of rural India is founded mainly on their functional specialisation and interdependence. For example, agriculture is the occupation of Kapu group of castes but all other castes—both high and low cultivate land if they have any, besides their traditional occupation. Similarly, the other castes also follow. Tradition has given to each group a definite position in the structure of the community and with that position goes a definite economic function which is the major source of livelihood for that group. There is not any traditional occupation for women.

Table-10 shows the occupation of the respondents. In our study, different occupations were found. They have been categorised into doctors, nurses, lecturers, teachers, clerks, technical assistants, attenders and sweepers.

Table 10
Occupation of the Respondents

Occupation of the respondents	*Number of respondents*	*Percentages*
Doctors	20	6.7
Nurses	15	5.0
Lectures (in Junior Degree and University colleges)	100	33.3
Teachers (in Primary and Secondary Schools)	92	30.7
Clerks, Stenographers	50	16.7
Technical Assistants	9	3.0
Attenders	7	2.3
Sweepers	7	2.3
Total	300	100.0

It is seen from the Table 10 that among different occupational groups, lecturers formed the largest group and their percentage constituted 33.33. They were found working in Junior, Degree and University colleges. The next larger group were teachers whose percentage was 30.70. On the whole, in our Sample, 64.03 per cent of the respondents belonged to teaching community, The remaining percentage was shared by respondents with different occupations. Interestingly, it was noticed from the information furnished by the respondents that a working woman found teaching profession as highly respectable and satisfactory. In addition, 16.7 per cent were clerks and stenographers working in banks and government offices. Doctors and nurses constituted 6.7 per cent and 5 0 per cent respectively. For a long time, Christians were doing the profession of nursing. Now their bias has been overcome and many of women from other communities are found employed as nurses in hospitals. There were technical assistants, sweepers and attenders in the sample and their percentages were 3.0, 2.3 and 2.3 respectively.

Monthly Income

Income is one of the important factors in the economic condition of working women. Income from other sources was excluded from the purview of calculation and analysis. While computing income, the respondents' income alone was taken into account.

Table 11 gives a picture of the income of the respondents religion-wise.

Table 11

Income Groups of the Respondents Religion-Wise

Income groups of the respondents per month in Rs.	*Hindus*	*Christians*	*Muslims*	*Total*
500-1000	112 (87.2)	8 (7.7)	6 (5.1)	126 (42.0)
1001-1500	67 (87.0)	10 (13.0)	—	77 (25.7)
1501-2000	53 (96.4)	1 (1.8)	1 (1.8)	55 (18.3)
2001-2500	26 (96.3)	1 (3.7)	—	(27) (9.0)
2501-3000	13 (86.7)	1 (6.7)	1 (6.7)	15 (5.0)
Total	271 (90.3)	21 (7.0)	8 (2.7)	300

The data shows that majority of the respondents were low-income groups. 67.7 per cent of the respondents' income was between Rs. 500/- and Rs. 1500/. In this category, technical assistants, sweepers, attenders, clerks and strenographers and nurses could be seen. While 18.3 per cent, 9 per cent and 5 per cent of the respondents belonged to the income groups, Rs. 1500/- to Rs. 2000/-, Rs. 2001/- to Rs. 2500/- and Rs. 2501/- to Rs. 3000/- respectively. In these income groups could be seen teachers, lecturers and doctors. Religion wise, majority of respondents belonging low income groups could be seen in all three communities. Of 21 Christian respondents, one each could be seen in Rs. 2001/- to Rs. 2500/- and Rs. 2500/- to Rs. 3000/- categories. Similarly, there was only one Muslim respondent in the income group of Rs. 2501/- to Rs. 3000/. The analysis points out that the income of the majority of the respondents was not high.

Table 12

Income-Wise Age Groups of the Respondents

Income groups of the respondents per month in Rs.	*15-20*	*21-30*	*31-40*	*41-50*	*51 and above*	*Total*
501-1000	1 (0.3)	5 (25.0)	4 (11.3)	7 (2.3)	9 (3.0)	26 (42.0)
1001-1500	—	36 (12.0)	31 (10.3)	8 (2.7)	2 (0.7)	77 (25.7)
1501-2000	—	12 (4.0)	29 (9.7)	6 (2.0)	8 (2.7)	55 (18.3)
2001-2500	—	1 (0.3)	10 (3.3)	10 (3.3)	6 (2.0)	27 (9.0)
2501-3000	—	1 (0.3)	3 (1.0)	7 (2.3)	4 (1.3)	15 (5.0)
Total	1 (0.3)	125 (41.7)	107 (35.7)	38 (19.7)	29 (12.7)	300

Age-wise, the data in Table 12 indicates that 41.7 per cent the respondents belonging to all income groups were aged between 21 and 30 years and 35.7 per cent between 31 and 40 years. Altogether 77.4 per cent of the respondents belonging to all categories of income were young. Whereas, 14.7 per cent respondents could be seen in the age group of 41-50 years. 12.7 per cent of the respondents' age was 51 years and above. Compared to the middle aged and old, the percentage of young working women was more.

Income and Literacy

Income varies according to the level of literacy. The higher the level of literacy the higher the level of income will be. The data in Table 13 illustrates this point clearly. 51.3 per cent and 21.7 per cent of the total respondents belonging to all categories of income were post-graduates and graduates. Only 8.3 per cent possessed technical and other professional qualifications. Whereas, 18.6 per cent of the respondents with school and Intermediate education could be seen in all income groups. Among the graduates and post-graduates, a greater number belonged to the low-income group. That is their income ranged between Rs. 500/- and Rs. 1500/-.

Reasons for taking up Job

Women enter into job market for various reasons. Of them, the chief reason being for the sake of economic gains and security. There may be other reasons like striving for power and prestige. In our study these reasons have not counted much significance. It has been found that 71.6 per cent of the respondents have taken up jobs for fulfilling economic gains and security. While 21.6 per cent and 6.7 per cent of the respondents cited the reasons as "support of family" and "for power and prestige" (see Table 14).

Thus, it is clear that the job selection by women in most of the cases has been governed by three major factors. These are to fulfil one's own economic gains and security, to support family and for the sake of power and prestige. Religion-wise,

Table 13
Income-Wise Educational Level of the Respondents

Income group of the respondents per month in Rs.	*Primary education*	*Secondary education*	*Matric/ Intermediate*	*Graduation*	*Post-graduation*	*Technical*	*Professional*	*Total*
501-1000	11 (8.70)	17 (13.60)	11 (8.70)	41 (33.40)	41 (33.40)	5 (2.02)	—	126 (42.0)
1001-1500	—	6 (7.8)	10 (13.0)	19 (24.7)	38 (49.4)	—	4 (5.2)	77 (25.7)
1501-2000	—	—	1 (1.8)	5 (9.1)	43 (78.2)	1 (1.8)	5 (9.1)	55 (18.3)
2001-2500	—	—	—	—	25 (92.6)	1 (3.7)	1 (3.7)	27 (9.0)
2501-3000	—	—	—	—	7 (46.7)	—	8 (53.3)	15 (5.0)
Total	11 (3.6)	23 (7.7)	22 (7.3)	65 (21.7)	154 (51.3)	7 (2.3)	18 (6.0)	300)

the data reveals that Hindu respondents figured in the above three specified reasons. Of which economic gains and security accounted 71.6 per cent. "To support the family" recorded 21.6 per cent, while "for power and prestige" a negligible per centage (6.7). In the case of Christians and Muslims, the respondents cited only two reasons namily, to support the family and for economic gains and security.

Table 14

Reason for Taking up Job

Religion	*Support the family*	*To fulfil the aspiration*	*For economic gains*	*For power and prestage*	*To spend time*	*Suits the qualification*	*Total*
Hindus	51 (18.81%)	—	200 (73.80%)	20 (7.38%)	—	—	271
Christians	8 (38.09%)	—	13 (61.90%)	—	—	—	21
Muslims	6 (75.0%)	—	2 (25.0%)	—	—	—	8
Total	65 (21.6%)	—	215 (71.6%)	20 (6.7%)	— —	— —	300

Husband's attitude towards Wife's Occupation

Marital harmony of the working women depends on several factors like the husband's acceptance of wife's participation in economic life. If the husband does not like it, then the domestic harmony is disturbed. Studies (Kapadia, 1959, Desai, 1957, Hate, 1948 and 1969, Rose, 1961, Cormack, 1961, Sengupta, (1960) have shown that there may be husbands who may like the economic participation of wife but not its consequences in the form of neglect of domestic duties and responsibilities of the form of neglect of domestic duties and responsibilities of the wife. Our study has also evaluated the husband's attitude towards wife's occupation from the working women respondents' point of view. The data is presented in the following Table 15.

Table 15

Husband's Attitude Towards Wife's Occupation
(According to the respondents)

Religion	*Most satisfied*	*Satisfied*	*Not satisfied*	*Total*
Hindus	150 (55.3%)	121 (44.7%)	—	271
Christians	16 (76.2%)	5 (23.8%)	—	21
Muslims	—	8 (100.0)	—	8
Total	166 (55.3)	134 (44.7)		300

It has been found in the study that 55.3 per cent of the total respondents expressed that thelr husbands were fully and most satisfied with their participation in job. While 44.7 per cent respondents said that their husbands were simply satisfied with their working outside home. No woman's husband expressed 'not satisfied'. Thus, it is clear that working women have the support and approval of their husbands in work participation.

Conflict between Job and Home Responsibilities

It is quite usual that working women face role-conflict in their day-to-day living. Since the domestic responsibilities demand heavy concentration on the part of working women, it invariably results in strain and stress on the one hand and the role conflict dilema on the other (Kala Rani, 1976 ; Kapur, 1974 : 29-30). Working women have to devote considerable time in the case of the old and sick persons in the upbringing of their children and the daily domestic chores. Inquiring into these aspects, the working women have been asked to state whether they had come across any conflict while discharging the responsibilities both in the office and in the house.

Table 16

Conflict Between Home and Job Responsibilities

Religion	*No conflict*	*Problem due to illness, old age and children's education*	*Non cooperative attitude of the colleagues*	*Excessive involvement in office work*	*Total*
Hindu	160 (59.04%)	59 (21.7%)	38 (14.02%)	14 (5.16%)	271
Christians	8 (38.09%)	5 (23,8%)	—	8 (38.09%)	21
Muslims	4 (50.0%)	3 (37.5%)	—	1 (12.5%)	8
Total	172 (57.3%)	67 (22.33%)	38 (12.66%)	23 (7.6%)	?00

It has been found in our study that 57.3 per cent respondents confessed that they had no conflict between job and home responsibilities. Whereas the remaining 42.7 per cent respondents faced various conflicting situations in home and work place. Among these, 22.3 per cent respondents faced conflicting situations because of illness, old age of parents and children's education. 12.66 per cent and 7.6 per cent respondents cited different problems like non-cooperative attitude of the colleagues and excessive involvement in office work.

Religion-wise, among Hindus a High percentage (59.04%) said they had no conflict between job and home responsibilities, while the remaining 41.06 per cent encountered various problems at home with childern and old people (21.7 per cent), in the office with their colleagues (14.02) per cent) and excessive involvement in office work (5.16 per cent). In respect of Christians and Muslims, none expressed any problems with with their colleagues in the office. No conflict recorded 38.09 per cent and 50.0 per cent respectively among Christians and Muslims. While excessive involvement of work in the office accounted 38.9 per cent and 12.5 per cent respectively among Christians and Muslims.

Savings

The progress of a nation is reflected in the savings of its people. The more the people save the healthier the nation would be. From ones savings, one can be assessed ones stan-

Table 17

Saving of the Respondents

Religion	*Yes*	*No*	*Total*
Hindus	256 (94.5%)	15 (5.5%)	271
Christians	18 (85.71%)	3 (14.28%)	11
Muslims	6 (75%)	2 (25.3%)	8
Total	280 (93.3%)	20 (6.7%)	300

dard of living. It is the barometer of one's living standards. Women hardly save in the rural areas. Whatever the meagre money they get would go into their daily domestic expenses. Compared to rural savings among women, urban women, it has been found, seem to save a little more. Particularly, working women save money for various reasons like to meet unforeseen expenses in future in respect of health, their daughter's marriage's their children's welfare and so on. While computing savings, the respondent's nature of savings alone was taken into consideration and not their respective husbands.

It has been found in our study that a greater majority of the respondents (93.3 per cent) save, while a negligible percentage of the respondents (6.7 per cent) do not. This shows that the habit of saving is more among working women. Religion wise, the data also points out the same trend. Not much difference could be seen among the Christian and Muslim respondents. Those who could not save were found to be sweepers, attenders and technical assistants. They could not save because their income was low and meagre. However, they expressed their eagerness to save provided their income position improved. While those who had the habit of saving included doctors, nurses, teachers and clerks. The mode of their savings was through commercial bank and LIC. They cited reasons like to meet expenses of their daughter's marriage in future, children's welfare and medical health.

Conclusion

It may be drawn from the preceding analysis and discussion that the family set-up of working women was totally changed. The traditional set-up of joint family was replaced by nuclear family. Data in table 6 and 7 testify this fact. 203 respondents out of 300 opted for nuclear family, which shows that there was a difinite change in the family pattern. However the extended family was still in vogue as was revealed from the survey that 82 respondents adhered to it. As a result of the changes in family structure, the status of woman in family was also affected. 270 respondents treated themselves equal to men.

They did not in any way feel inferior to men. Both men and women equally took part in all important domestic affairs.

Education is an important indicator of social status of women. Education is directly proportional to the status of women. Majority of respondents had higher educational qualificalions. 154 respondents (51.3 per cent) were post-graduates and 65 graduates (see Table 8). We also find women possessed professional qualifications. 25 respondents were professional. It may be found that women with higher educational qualifications sought employment outside. They were more eager to take up tough jobs, both technical and non-technical. Thus, education is an important facter that brings change in the status and position of woman in the society.

It may be further seen that majority of the respondents from the upper castes had higher educational qualifications. of 210 respondents belonging to various Forward castes like Kapu, Kamma, Brahmin, Kshatriya, Balija, Naidu, Nair, Vysya and Maharashtra Brahmin, a higher proportion possessed graduate and post-graduate qualifications. Whereas among the Backward cast working women, a lesser percentage of educational qualifications was noticed. However, on the whole, an overwhelming majority of the respondents possessed higher educational qualifications.

To sum up the economic composition of the respondents, it may be seen that among Muslims a few women were employed. Traditionally, they are not allowed to work outside the home. On the other hand, Christian women were found employed in all sectors both private and public and their number was higher than the Muslim working women. The majority of respondents were Hindus. As for reasons for taking up job, majority of the respondents (71.6 per cent) cited the reason as to fulfil economic gains and security. To support family (21.6 per cent) and for power and prestige (6.7 per cent) were also reasoned out. Higher education facilitated women's entry into gainful employment. This is more true of the middle class women. The Hindu women have come out from the clutches of traditional values and slowly started joining the work-force. Their participation in work-force has considerably led to the improvement of their social position and status. Nevertheless, their increasing participation in the economic activity is very essential for India's growth and progress.

In respect of income, majority of the respondents belonged to low-income groups. High income could be seen among doctors and lecturers. Further, most of the respondents in the low income group were graduates and post-graduates. Education-wise majority of the working women possessed higher qualifications.

Matrimonial harmony prevailed. Husband's attitude towards wife taking up job outside home has been found to be positive and encouraging. Majority of the respondent's husband (55.3 per cent), on assessment, were most satisfied with their wives participating in work outside home. There were no husbands who were unsatisfied or dissatisfied. Similarly, with regard to the conflict role, majority of the respondents (57.3 per cent) confessed that they had no conflict roles between their work and home responsibilities. However, the remaining 42.7 per cent expressed that they had been facing various conflicting situations both at home and in the office, resulting in stress and strain on their psyche. In respect of their saving habits an overwhelming majority of the respondents (93.3 per cent) answered positively. This shows that the working women save on their own to meet the unforeseen expenditure.

3

Rites of Passage

Introduction

Ritual is defined as a technique to manipulate the supernatural power. It is a series of rites related to a body of beliefs through which the mind is transformed and purified. The rituals may be classified into group crises and rites of passage on the basis of their periodic and non-periodic occurences (Van Gennep 1908, Junod 1913, Chaple and Coon 1942).

It is interesting to note that while periodical rituals are performed in terms of community-wide festivals and celebrations which mostly reveal the communal impact, the non-periodical rituals, such as rites of passage reveal the anxious moments in an individual's life and their importance to the family group. The non-periodical rituals are those occasional rites largely linked up with domestic events or life cycle ceremonies such as birth, marriage and death. Recognising the social importance of non-periodical rituals, Gannep[1] interprets these events as a transition from one social status to another and he termed these rituals as Rites of Passage. According to him, the rituals connected with this nature are composed of three consecutive elements : separation, transition and reintegration.

In almost all societies rituals are practised in one way or another. In no culture they are ignored. They are considered to be vital to the well-being of the individual, the family, the group and the community. In India Hindu women attach great importance to rituals. According to the Hindu mythology, a house-holder has to observe certain important rituals during the life span. But, normally those which are essential during life crisis are observed. These rituals start when the child is in the womb and end with the death ceremonies. There is no fixed day or month or year to perform these non-periodical rituals. These rituals are individual or family-oriented rather than community-oriented.

Pregnancy

The first life cycle ceremony starts with pregnancy. Hindu believe that without the blessings of God and ancestral spirits no woman would be able to conceive though they are aware of the causal connection between sexual intercourse and conception. Working women too have such beliefs. If menstruation stops for two or three months it is an indication of conception. When a woman is certain of her pregnancy she informs her mother-in-law. A Hindu welcomes the birth of a baby as it is a sign of the expansion of his/her family.

Like others, the pregnant working woman is taken away from her conjugal place when she reaches the seventh or eigth month of her first pregnancy. In this month, the parents of the pregnant woman visit their daughter at her husband's residence and offer certain gifts to her consisting of new clothes, vermillion and a small quantity of turmeric tubers. All the relatives and friends are invited to take part in this ritual bath with not water and the mother presents her new clothes. All the elderly women in the assembly bless her on the occasion. Like other Hindu women, the pregnant working woman also touches the feet of all elderly ladies for blessings. This ritual ceremony is called as 'Seemantham'.

During the pregnancy period, she observes many restrictions not only to herself but to the growing child in the womb.

She is also not allowed to eat papaya fruit and the black coloured fruits like nerudu (Engine jambolana) for the reason that the offspring may be black.

The pregnant lady along with her parents worships family deity for easy delivery before it. The backward castes like Yadavas, Gandla, Besta, Odde and Jangam worship some of the local deities such as Muneswarudu, Akkagarulu, Parentalu and Kateri. Similarly the Harijan working women worship their own Inti Devathale or Grama Devathalu before delivery.

It is learnt that the Hindu working women observe this ritual in the fifth or seventh or in the ninth month. Out of 271 Hindu respondents, 151 working women observe this ritual and the remaining 120 avoid it for economic reasons. All Muslim working women (8) and Christian working (21) women also observe this ceremony.

Child Birth

As soon as an elederly woman detects the signs of delivery, the working woman performs a ritual in order to propropitiate the ancestral deities and offerings to the great traditional Sanskritic deities for easy and safe delivery. Pollution is observed for a period of eleven or thirteen days. The newborn child is given a bath in warm water and the fumes of benzoic powder are used to protect the child's body. The Hindu custom requires a confined woman to observe pollution for thirteen days during which she is not supposed to touch others or anything in the house. She is forbidden from approaching the domestic deity. After the delivery the mother is given food on the third day. The Hindu working women observe it strictly for they think that if the mother is allowed to take certain types of food, the health of the child is bound to be affected. On the thirteenth day after the cofinement the subject takes a ritual purificatory bath. Relatives and friends attend the function on invitation. The entire house is decorated. The mother and the child take oil bath. After the bath, the mother is given a special decoction to protect her from ill-health.

All the Hindu working women irrespective of their caste differences follow the ritual bath with a special ceremonial worship. With this process, the mother of the child gets purified and thus is allowed to move freely. With the bath on the thirteenth day, the mother becomes pure. She then cooks food for the first time after confinement. The purification ceremony day is a day of domestic ceremony and a lamp is lighted before the domestic deity. After delivery, the working woman does not indulge in sexual intercourse until the child attains the age of three months

Tonsure Ceremony

The Hindu working women also perform the tonsure ceremony generally when the baby attains the age of nine months or completes the first year or in some cases in the third year. The child's maternal uncle plays an important role in this act. The woman and her husband fix an auspicious day for the ceremony and intimate it to the maternal uncle of the child. On the morning of the auspicious day, the mother invites the awomenfolk and the relatives.

The lady gives a bath to the child in warm water and puts a vermillion mark on its forehead. A wooden plank is arranged in the outer verandah of the house under which some paddy and copper coins are placed. After the child is seated on the plank, the maternal uncle clips with scissors the hair of the child at five places around the head. Next the barber is asked to a clean shave. Like the other Hindus, the working women prohibit others from touching the hair as it is considered unclean and polluted, an item breeding infection and skin diseases. Once again the child is given a bath in warm water. After the purificatory bath the child wears the new clothes presented by maternal uncle. Then the maternal uncle takes bath. A feast usually follows the ritual. The barber is also presented with food provisions besides a little cash for the services he renders on the occasion.

The most significant change of this ceremony is that the presence of maternal uncle is not made compulsory. Among the Hindu working women, there are however no special elaborate ritual ceremonies being observed to mark the occassions of piercing the ears and noses of the female and male children. For all female children the piercing of ears and noses is done in the eleventh month.

First Puberty of First Menstruation Ceremony

The Hindu working women observe ceremonies when girls menstruate for the first time. The event is called as 'Peddamanishi Kavadamu'. Puberty ceremony marks the beginning of adolescence. When a girl gets her first menstruation, a word is sent to her paternal aunt. The family members bring green leaves and place them evenly over the paddy grains spread on the floor for the occassion. On the first day, the girl's mother invites other womenfolk for the occassion. In the presence of all ladies, the girl is seated on the leaves. The lady of the house offers kumkum and distributes 'akshantalu' (rice soaked in turmeric paste) to all ladies. All women bless the girl by sprinkling the akshantalu on her head. Later the sweet made of gingerly seeds and jaggery is distributed to all relatives and friends present at the function.

During the period of seclusion the girl is provided with a mat and a pillow and asked to sit and sleep in particular place in the house. She is not expected to move out. She is strictly forbidden to enter into the kitchen. In all her movements she is guided by her paternal aunt who also does the job of serving food.

On the morning of the last day of the period of seclusion the girl's mother invites all relatives and friends and neighbours. No male member is allowed to take part in the ceremony. In the meantime, the girl's paternal aunt cleans the place where the girl spends her seclusion and then is duly decorated. As all women gather, the girl is taken to the backyard of the house and is seated on wooden plank and smeared with turmeric powder and is given a hot water oil bath. After ritual bath the girl is exposed to the fumes of the benzoic powder. Later she is given new apparel to wear, preferably yellow. All women who attend the function clean their hands and faces with turmeric water. They bless the girl and wish her a happy and bright future by sprinkling the aksjantalu on her head. The feast follows.

So far as the first menstruation is concerned all Hindu working women observe the rituals with no distinctions. However, no special ceremonies are observed during the subsequent menstruations. Due to modernisation and secularisation some among working women, do not maintain any seclusion for a period of three days. Instead, they take bath immediately after menstruation and attend all domestic activities. In the case of nuclear families no elder woman is present for guiding the girl. This indicates the total rejection of traditional practices in the observance of menstruation.

Upanayana Ceremony

While puberty ceremony is for girls, the Upanayana ceremony is meant for boys. Among Hindu working women orthodox castes like Brahmins, Visva Brahmins, Kshtriyas, Nairs and Nysyas perform the intiation ceremony for the boys as they attain adulthood. The Brahmin priest officiates over the ritual. Generally, this ceremony takes place in the months of February, March, April, May and June. With the consultation of an astrologer, the boy's father fixes an auspicious day for the ceremony. On this day the householder invites all relatives and friends. The boy is subjected to purificatory ritual bath followed by worship of domestic deities by offering sacred food. He is neatly shaved and annointed with oil and finally given a purificatory bath. After the ritual bath under the spells of vedic hymns, the parents adore the shoulders of the boy with the sacred thread. All the invitees bless the boy and offer him gifts. Now the boy is fully entitled to take part in socio-religious functions and ceremonies. Until the boy is subjected to Upanayana, he is considered a Sudra, and an orthodox Brahmin will not allow his son to eat with him. From the day of the initiation ceremony, the boy is expected to pray to Gayatri Devi, the Goddess of prosperity, twice a day.

Every year the cord is to be replaced by a new one in the months of July and August. This festival is known as 'Sravanalapaurnavami' the full moon in the month of Sravana (July-August). The performance of this periodical duty obtains for the individual the remission of all sins committed during the year. Some lower communities like Jangam and Yadava working women are also observing this ceremony in order to achieve high social status.

Marriage

Marriage is an important aspect of human life. Marriage and family are the basic institutions of society. As an institution it admits men and women to family life. Westermart defines marriage as a "more or less durable connection between male and female, lasting beyond the mere act of procreation..."[2] According to Lundberg, marriage consists of "the rules and regulations which define the rights, duties and privileges of husband and wife, with respect to each other."[3] Mazumdar observes ' as a socially sanctioned union of male and female, or as a secondary institution devised by society to sanction the union and mating of male and female, for purposes of (a) establishing a household, (b) entering into sex relation, (c) procreating and (d) providing care of the offspring."[4]

Hindus regard marriage not only as a social necessity but a sacrament and it involves rites which are strictly followed it accordance with the custom and tradition, though there are variations from caste to caste, family to family and sub caste. The three traditionally accepted aims of marriage are Dharma, Praja and Rati.

In all societies, pre-puberty marriages are almost non-existent and unacceptable. Marriage is permissible between a set of relatives belonging to certain gotras. Among Hindus the arranged marriage by parents is more popular and acceptable. The social part of the marriage ceremony is far more elaborate than the ritual and religious part. A boy is obliged to marry the daughter of his maternal uncle as a matter of duty. Similarly, the girl is obliged to marry the son of her maternal uncle. It is one of the important characteristic features of the South Indian Society.

Whenever a family wants to go in for a girl other than the cross-cousin and uncle niece marriage, the girl is seen before hand by the parents of the boy along with a mediator on an auspicious day fixed by the priest. The negotiations are traditionally prolonged. In fact, the fixation ceremony is an elaborate process. On an auspicious day fixed by the priest, the parents and the maternal uncle of the boy proceed to the house of the girl with flowers and fruits. On their arrival the bride's parents conduct them into the house and then are seated at their respective seats.

The elders of the bride's family and friends will be present. The bride dressed with her new clothes and ornaments is brought and presented to the party. One of the elders of the groom's party puts some questions to the bride. During the course of conversation, the members of the groom's party try to evaluate the personality of the girl. This is the traditional form of selecting the bride. After accepting the proposal, the groom's party will have negotiations on dowry with the elders of the bride. Dowry is prevailing among working women. Even though the girl is an earning member, dowry is a must for her. After having settled the dowry, the groom's party fixes a day for the betrothal ceremony. The party first visits the bride's residence with presents. On their arrival, the bridegroom and the bride will be seated side by side. After performing the 'Gowri Puja' the groom's parents present a saree and ornament to the bride who wears them and seeks blessing from the elders. The relatives and friends assist in the party.

After the proposal and betrothal, an auspecious date, time and place is fixed for celebrating the public event. All the members of the family, relatives and friends attend the funcion and participate in it with gaiety and enthusiasm. Generally, the working women conduct marriages in kalyana mandapams specially run by the Tirumala Tirupati Devastanams either at Tirupati or on the hills. Before muhurtam, they observe some preliminary ritual ceremonies such as nail-cutting and ritual bath.

In the nail-cutting ceremony, the barber removes the nails of fingers and toes of the bride. This ceremony is called as the Virgin-nail ceremony'. It is observed by all communities. Now-a-days the Forward Caste working women do not observe this ceremony for they cosider it highly traditional and conservative. However, the Backward Caste and Scheduled Caste working women still practise it at the time of marriages.

Yet another ceremony that precedes muhurtam is 'Kankanam ceremony'. A Kankanam is a band of peepul or mango leaves tied to a thread. The groom ties the bracelet (kanakanam) to the left wrist of the groom. Thereafter, the pair is strictly prohibited from attending any household duties for a period of three to five days until the kanakanams are removed. Then the couple is given a purificatory ritual bath and new clothes are offered to them to wear. After they are dressed, their feet are decorated with turmeric solution and vermillion powder which is essential for all spouses in order to ward off evil spirits or evil eyes. The Hindu working women observe this ritual.

Kanyadana ceremony is another important in the process of marriage. Both bride and groom are seated on a yoke facing each other. Two sacred tiny discs (pustic) tried to a thread, necklace of black beads, silver toe rings and some other ornaments are placed on a plate. While the drums are being beaten, at the fixed auspicious moment, the groom fastens the sacred tail to the neck of the girl. Later he ties the necklace of black beads to the bride. One of the ladies beloging to the groom's family fixes a toe ring to the second toe of each of leg of the bride.

These are the symbols of the married women. This ritual is considered sacred for all Hindus. Then the 'rite of seven steps' (Saptapadi) takes place. The husband makes the wife step forward in a northern direction seven steps with the words, one step for sap, two for juice; three for the prospering of wealth, four for comforts, five for cattle, six for seasons and the seven for unification. The objects referred to in the above formula are essential for domestic felicities. This ceremony is very important from the legal point of view, as marriage is regarded legally complete only after it has been performed. The feast follows the ceremony in which all relatives and friends take part.

After the feast bride is ceremoniously handed over to the care of the groom and his parents in the presence of elderly persons. After the marriage, at present, there is no special ritual function for nuptials. However, the couple leads an independent life in a house of their own, independent of their respective parents.

All Hindu working women follow and observe all rituals associated with marriage though in a simplified manner. Expenditure is minimised.

Among Muslim respondents it is learnt that in accordance with Islamic traditions and customs with some regional and local modifications. No significant change among the Christian marriages has been noticed. They too are strictly following their own traditions and customs. Thus, it may be noted that the Muslim and Christian working women follow their age-old traditions in conformity to their religion.

Death Ceremonies

All Hindus believe in the inevitability of death. For them death results in the departure of soul from the body. At his departure from this world, his survivours consecrate his death for his future felicity in the next world. Funeral rituals are performed in the memory of the departed soul. It also serves as an occasion for gathering of kith and kin.

It is believed that the departed soul must be honoured more than the living being with all necessary ritual pomp and show. The death ceremony involves huge expenditure. It is ensured by all the relatives that no one avoids performing the ritual. Working women are not exceptional in observing these ritual practices. Hindus perform funeral rites in two different stages. The minor funeral ceremony takes place on the third day immediately after the death of a person. The Hindus call this as 'Chinnadinamulu'. It is followed by the major (final) ceremony on the eleventh day. The Hindus firmly believe that the final funeral ceremony symbolises a complete severence of all earthly connections between the departed individual and the members of the surviving family.

The Hindu working women also observe a long series of rituals. As soon as the death of a person occurs elders of the family convey the sad news to all relatives and friends. The eldest son of the family plays a prominent role in funeral ceremonies. The Hindus keep the dead body on a wooden bamboo ladder with its head facing the south. The corpse is kept in the living room of the house or outside the varandah for a day or two in order to facilitate the relatives and friends to pay their last respects to the departed soul. It is obligatory on the part of relatives to attend the function. Until the body is removed for cremation, the entire family observes pollution, during which time, the food is cooked and served by the nearest relatives or in some cases by neighboures. On the evening or the next day the eldest son moves the body out of the house. Later it is throughly washed with water. After the ritual bath the corpse is dressed in new clothes and laid on the wooden ladder with a new cloth covering it.

At the same time, the living partner of the deceased is also given a ritual bath. The caste people make a selection of six or eight pall-bearers from their own caste. No one whose wife is pregnant or is in monthly periods or in confinement and also who has father and mother alive is eligible to act as a pall-bearer. Among the lower caste's women except those who are in pregnancy or in monthly periods or under confinement follow men to the cremation or burial ground. In the absence of the eldest son, his next successor leads the funeral procession. If the deceased is a woman, her husband who is alive will perform the rituals. In the absence of the husband, the son will conduct the funeral ceremonies. In the case of the death of a man, his surviving son or the nearest agnate will perform the rituals.

A pit, south-north, nine feet long, four feet wide and three feet deep is dug and kept ready under supervision of the elders. After performing some rites, the body is then lowered into the pit and covered with mud. In some cases, the dead body is placed on firewood with its head towards south and it is covered with a large quantity of firewood piled three to five feet above the ground level. The subject first lits fire to the leaves and later to the pyre. The body is slowly consigned to flames and ashes.

The party returns to the home of the deceased family. Every member is expected to take a ritual bath before he or she enters the house. An elderly woman kindles a sacred lamp and places it in the house. It is kept on burning throughout the polluting period.

On the morning of the third day the chief performer of the ceremony goes to the cremation ground to collect the bones and ashes of the dead. After collecting some bones and ashes, the subject pours some milk on the spot. This ritual ceremony is called as 'Palu poyadamu'. Later the subject returns home and takes the ritual bath. The vessel containing bones and ashes is kept in the sacred place of the house for some days. Later they are immersed in a river.

During the pollution which lasts for eleven days, the spouse of the deceased is expected to take bath daily. Every day at ihe beginning of each meal the cooked food is to be first offered to the domestic deity and to the departed soul.

On the eleventh day morning, the entire house is cleaned and decorated in a traditional manner. Every surviving member of the deceased family takes a purificatory ritual bath in order to attain the normal ritual status. After the ritual ceremony the first grade mourners, that is the children of the deceased, sons and their wives, are allowed to move freely in the house. All the relatives attend the function. The subject on this day offers food and milk to the departed soul. Hindus believe that this item of the ritual turns the ancestral spirits to be cordial to the new departed soul into their fold. The maternal uncle presents new clothes to the performer and also to the spouse of the deceased.

Among Forward Castes, Brahmins, Nairs, Vysyas and Maharashtra Brahmins burn the dead. The other Forward Castes like Kapu, Kamma, Balija and Naidu bury the dead. Some of the lower castes like Bestha, Gandla, Yadav cremate the dead. Rajaka, Kummara and Karanam bury the dead. However, the children below fifteen years of age are buried in all castes including the twice-born communities.

The ritual ceremonies for Muslims and Christians differ. The Muslims generally take the dead first to the mosque where a funeral service called Namay-e-Janaya is conducted and later the dead body is burried with its head placed towards north and the face turned to the west in the direction of Mecca. The Christians also take the dead to the Church for the funeral service before burial in the ceremony.

Widowhood Ceremony

Before the feast on the final funeral ceremony day, a special ceremony takes place to declare the wife of the deceased as a widow. All women other than the widows are prohibited from attending the ceremony. The ritual is conducted by the priest. The performer of the funeral is called upon the break the bangles, black beads, the sacred pustie and other ornaments of the widow. Among Hindus a widow is expected to observe certain taboos. She is not supposed to wear coloured sarees. She is forbidden to apply vermillion mark on her forehead. However, these restrictions are not strictly followed by widows. Now they wear bangles, sarees of varied colours and put vermillion marks. They move freely without restriction.

Conclusions

After having examined various rituals and ceremonies it

may be concluded that the Hindu working women follow and observe various rituals and ceremonies during the times of crises though in a simplified manner. The rites of passage serve the purpose of adjusting men and women to the crisis situation by showing a way for emotional security.

Some important changes in ritual practices associated with the life cycle ceremonies may be noted. The working women do not observe the period of pollution during menstruation, because of their involvement in their jobs Immediately after menstruation they take oil bath and attend their domestic duties. They rarely worship deities. All respondents perform the most important rites connected with the birth and growth of the child. Brahmins, Kshatriyas, Nairs, Vysayas, Maharashtra Brahmin and Viswa Brahmins invite priests for the naming ceremony. The other caste working women conduct the ceremony without the help of the priest. No respondent stictly observes 'Annaprasana' ceremony (giving food to the baby in the seven month). The usual feasting associatea with such ceremonies is often omitted due to the absence of caste community members or other sympathetic people. Nevertheless simple ceremonies are performed with less expenditure, but the necessary rituals take place.

Similarly rituals associated with marriages are simplified. They are celebrated with less pomp and show. Simple feasts are arranged. However, it depends on the economic status of a family. Dowry is accepted. Kapus, Kammas, Naidus and Kshatriyas pay enormous dowry. The lower caste working women pay less or more dowry depending on their economic position. Brahmins, Viswa Brahmins and Maharashtra Brahmin pay less dowry.

The death and after rites are carried out when necessary by all. However, the after death ceremonies depend on the links with the extended family. Where such links exist, traditional practices are adhered to. It is perhaps necessary to point out that the lavishness with which these ceremonies are performed has diminished.

Several rites associated with widowhood ceremony have been affected with changes. As against the past traditions, widows wear coloured sarees. One Brahmin and two Kapus are widows. They wear colour sarees, bangles, jewellery and flowers. They move freely in the society. They take part in all socio-cultural functions. Widow-remarriage is in vogue. Two widows from Kapu and Balija are remarried.

Several factors have contributed to the changes in the attitude of working women towards rituals associated with the life cycle ceremonies. Among them are urbanisation, modernisation, the spread of education, mass-media and occupational changes. Since women have been employed they are compelled to discharge dual role—the family role and occupational role. These two roles require scheduling and rescheduling the time for them. The woman's dual role is the result of the progressive change in socio-economic status. With the participation of a married woman in activities outside the home, certain changes have come in their attitude towards the practice and observance of rituals and rites in their day-to-day life.

References

1. Malefijit, Anne, M. : *Religion and Culture*, 1968, p. 190.
2. Westmark, Edward, : *Origin and Development of Moral Ideas*, 1964, Vol. II, p. 364.
3. Lundberg, G.A. : *Foundations of Sociology*. 1960, p. 133.
4. Masumdar, H.T. : *The Grammar of Sociology*, 1966, p. 582.

4

Religious Organisation

Religion comprises a systematic pattern of beliefs, practices and values. These aıe as old as human thought. They satisfy some psychological needs of human beings. They are widespread in all societies. Despite the remarkable expansion of knowledge and the great advances of science and technology, religious beliefs and practices continue to profit in people's lives. Religion is important because it codifies and expresses the cultural values of society as a whole. It is one of the agencies of social control. It gives guidelines for conduct and defines the ends and means in human affairs, human relations and human into reactions. As Durkheim rightly observes, religious beliefs and practice unite into one single more community called church all those who believe in it (Durkheim, Emile, 1957 : 47).

Hinduism is mainly based on the theory of Karma, the reincarnation of "soul". Hinduism postulates that the soul is liberated from the body with death and the soul thereafter may, for sometime reside in space and or enjoy heaven or suffer hell before it reincarnates in some form on earth, or may not have rebirth at all if its liberation from the body is complete. This eternal release of the soul from the body is called 'Salvation' or 'Moksha' or 'Mukti' or the union of the soul with God.

Hindus also believe that karma is a law of action and reaction, good or bad, that traces the present to the past. They also believe that the good deeds which the individual does, secures for him heaven or good things of life and that evil actions expose him to punitive consequences. The main goal of Hindus is to obtain 'Moksha'. The same religious tenet is also applicable to Islam and Christian religions. The difference lies in the worship of God and the goal of all the three religions is one, that is, how to attain or reach the Bliss of God. To obtain moksha both men and women perform several rites and rituals.

Man alone cannot perform certain rites and rituals without the participation of his life partner, wife. Hinduism has never been static. From time to time, innumerable saints, sages and philosophers appeared and reformed Hinduism by interpreting it in a right spirit and understanding. During the Middle ages the great religious and spiritual leaders like Ramunuja, Sankara, Madhva, Kablr, Tulsidas, Mira Bai, Bhakta Tukaram, Purandharadas, Basava Ramananda and Chaithanya protected our religion, culture and society from the onslaughts of alien hordes. In Nineteenth Century, mahy reformist movements like Brahma Samaj, Arya Samaj, Theosophical society and Ramakrishna Mission emerged and reformed and purified Hindu society. M.N. Srinivas (Srinivas, M.N., 1952 : 214-19) broadly divides Hinduism into four divisions namely All India Hinduism, Peninsular Hinduism, Regional Hinduism and local Hinduism.

1. *All India Hinduism*

It is chiefly sanscritic and spread in two ways. One is by the extension of sanscritic dieties and ritual forms to an outlaying group. The other is by the greater sanscritisation of the rituals and beliefs of the groups inside Hinduism.

2. *Peninsular Hinduism*

It is an area of enormous cultural diversities but it forms a dishevelled unity in relation to continental India. Certain ritual and cultural forms are found widespread even in Peninsular India. The Tali or marriage badge tied by the groom to the bride is found everywhere except among Coorgs in South India. The ritual practices and deities shared in common with Kannadigs and Tamilians usually come under Peninsular Hinduism.

3. *Regional Hinduism*

It often contains some sanscritic elements directly stressing regional ties, indirectly all India ties. The identification of Lord Subramanya Swamy with cobra among Coorgs, Thulus, Telugus and Kannadigas is significant. Cobras are worshipped throughout India by Hindus but their identification with Lord Subramanya Swamy is confined to certain areas in Peninsular Hinduism.

4. *Local Hinduism*

It is more restricied than regional Hinduism. The people of a village share a great many ritual and cultural forms in common, through membership of a caste frequently cuts across these alignments in the case of top and immigrant castes.

Hindu working women are by nature more religious and devotional than men. They periodically visit temples with great regularity, performed sacred rites with firm faith and observe religious fasts with more alacrity than men. Except during the periods of menstruation and confinement, women are regarded unpolluted by religion. During menstruational periods, the Hindu working women however attend their domestic and non-domestic duties without observing pollution except they worship family deities. After purificatory bath, women worship the family deities. The change is due to the impact of employment and to some extent their individual families.

Although women are excluded from the practice of Hindu priesthood particularly at the great traditional deities, they enthusiastically take part in important ceremonies, festivals and rituals at home and in temples. Women perform the rituals to see the protection and well-being of crucial kinsmen (especially husband and children), the general prosperity and the health of family members. Unmarried women perform rituals for good husbands.

Hindu religious activity is not solely based on Vedic rituals. Today the dominant form of ritual activity is bhakti or devotion to the deity. Performing puja (devotional ritual) is the principle form of ritual activity among Hindus in India. Hindus, irrespective of their caste and community, observe fast, celebrate festivals, vrates and religious functions, follow rituals, customs and practices and visit important pilgrimage centres.

Belief in God

Although belief in God (Divine) is strong throughout India, working women perhaps even more than men are devout believers in the supernatural. From the rites and ritual practices of the Hindus one can infer that they firmly believe in the existence of various deities associated with great and little traditional levels, souls of the departed ancestors and some cultural heroes of the Hindu mythology. All the deities are believed to be benevolent. Spirits are said to be both benevolent and malevolent but no significant names as such are given to them. Generally, the souls of the departed are considered benevolent. The four village deities propitiated by the Hindu working women are Gangamma, Veshalamma, Mutyalamma and Pothu Raju. The first three are female deities and Pothu Raju is a male deity. In addition to village deities, Hindu working women also worship the trinities—Lord Brahma, the creator, Lord Vishnu, the protector and Lord Siva, the destroyer and others such as Lord Vinayaka, Lord Anjaneya, Lord Subramanya, Lord Ayyappa, etc. Rituals associated with the propitiation of many of these deities are mainly collective and periodic in nature. The ancestor spirits are invoked and worshipped by individual families and the festivals are collectively and periodically celebrated (i.e., domestic group oriented) for the welfare of the whole community or society.

Hindu deities can be broadly categorised into two groups.

The first consists of purely local Gods and Goddesses and the second, the Gods and Goddesses derived from the Hindu sans-criticised literature and mythology.

The former however have close resemblances with the Peninsular region in general and surrounding plains of Telugu region in particular. In the latter category are included the deities such as Lord Ganapati, Lord Vishnu, Lord Brahma, Lord Siva, Lord Ayyappa, etc. The belief in earth mother is also associated with Hindu mythology.

For the purpose of worship, the Hindu working women have three principle deities – the Gramadevata (the Goddess of the villlage), the Kuladevata (the tutelary deity of the family and the Ista devata (personal deity). The first two are fixed by birth and the third is selected by the women from many deities of the Hindu Pantheon. Besides, an orthodox Hindu working woman worships many other deities.

Table 1

Belief in God Religion-wise

Religion of respondents	*Belief in God*		
	Yes	*No*	*Total*
Hinduism	233 (86.0)	38 (14.0)	271 (90.3)
Islam	8 (100.0)	–	8 (2.7)
Christianity	21 (100.0)	—	21 (7.0)
Total	262 (87.3)	38 (12.7)	300

The Muslim working women believe in Allah, the only God in Muhammad, the Holy Prophet as His messenger, while the Christian working women in one God i.e., Jesus Christ. Based on their beliefs, these two communities are termed as monotheists while the Hindus pantheists.

The Table 1 reveals that out of 271 Hindu respondents, 86 per cent believed in God whereas 14 per cent did not. All Christians and Muslim respondents expressed their faith in God. It may be deduced that there were no atheists among Christian and Muslim respondents, whereas among Hindus, division could be seen, theists and the atheists.

Belief in Forms of God

Table 2 gives a picture of beliefs in forms of God according to different age groups.

In respect of forms of God, different opinions persisted among the respondents. According to Table 2, out of 300 respondents 189 (62.9 per cent) believed that God has a structural and physical form, 61 respondents (20.4 per cent) affirmed that God has no form and the remaining 50 (16.7 per cent) asserted that they knew neither the form nor formlessness of the God. Religion-wise, among the total 271 Hindu respondents, 53.3 per cent believed that God has form, 20.4 per cent that God has no form and 16.7 per cent expressed neither. Age-wise, certain variations could be seen. Among those 160 Hindu respondents who confessed faith in God, 43.8 per cent were in the age group of 21-30 years and 35 per cent in 31-40 years. On the whole, majority of the believers were young and middle-aged. Only one Hindu respondent in the age group of 15-20 years responded that God has neither shape nor form. The data, however, reveals the fact that an overwhelming majority of the respondents irrespective of their religion and age variations expressed their sincere faith in God which has form and shape.

Belief in Idol Worship

Idol worship is popularly believed to be one of the most important aspects of Hindu religion. A Hindu regards the idol as a representation of God. An idol may be made of mud, stone or any metal such as bronze, silver, gold or panchaloha—

Table 2
Belief in Forms of God—Age-wise

Belief in forms of God	*Religion of the respondents*	*Age Group of the respondents in years*					*Total*
		15—20	*21—30*	*31—40*	*40—50*	*51 & above*	
God has form	Hinduism	—	70 (43.8)	56 (35.0)	17 (10.6)	17 (10.6)	160 (53.3)
	Islam	—	3 (37.5)	3 (37.4)	1 (12.5)	1 (12.5)	8 (2.6)
	Christianity	—	10 (47.6)	9 (42.9)	1 (4.6)	1 (4.8)	21 (7.0)
Formless	Hinduism	1 (1.6)	24 (39.3)	18 (29.5)	9 (14.8)	9 14.8)	61 (20.4)
	Islam	—	—	—	—	—	—
	Christianity	—	—	—	—	—	—
Don't know	Hinduism	—	18 (36.0)	21 (42.0)	10 (20.0)	1 (20.0)	50 (16.7)
	Islam	—	—	—	—	—	—
	Christianity	—	—	—	—	—	—
Total		1 (0.3)	125 (41.7)	107 (37.7)	38 (12.7)	29 (9.7)	300

a mixed metal composed of five ingredients copper, zinc, lead, tin, and iron. More often a paper on which the figure of God is painted is encased in a frame and worshipped. As there are many Gods in the Hindu pantheon, the idols which the Hindu worships are also many. Usually, a place or a room known as the pooja room is kept apart for the idols. A Hindu usually does 'pooja' in this room only. Among the many idols which may be present in the pooja room a particular deity such as Lord Venkateswara or Lord Shiva might be given prominance as it is regarded as family deity.

Table 3
Belief in Idol Worship

Religion of the Respondents	*Yes*	*No*	*Total respondents*
Hindus	271	–	271
Christians	21	–	21
Muslims	–	8	8
Total	292 (97.3%)	8 (2.7%)	390 (100.0%)

While all 271 Hindu respondents and 21 Christians (97.3 per cent) believed in idol worship, the 8 Muslim respondents (2.7 per cent) did not believe in it (see Table 3). All the 300 respondents however answered affirmatively that the remember God on all appropriate occasions.

With regard to membership in religious organisations, nearly 15 Hindu respondents had membership in organisations like Chinnaya Mission, Ramakrishan Mutt and Satya Sai Seva Samiti. The others did not have membership in any religious organisation or association. This, however, does not prove the fact that the working women are not deeply religious. The reasons for their non-membership and non-association with religious organisations may be attributed, as obtained from the respondents views, to their unwillingness to be associated, lack of time due to their working nature and their simple attitude of being indifferent.

Festivals

Festivals are occasions of great rejoicing and they are a part of religious life. They are celebrated all over the world, though they differ in their nature according to religion, culture, customs and traditions of the people of various countries. In India, almost all festivals are more or less common for al Hindus though they differ among the Shaivites and the Vaishnavites. For instance, majority of the Vaishnavites do not celebrate the festival of Lord Ganapati for the reason that it is connected with the cult of Lord Siva. However, throughout the Indian sub-continent, all Hindus observe all festivals except in a few cases. For example, the Holi and Raksha Bandan are celebrated throughout the Northern part of India with gaiety and fun while in the Southern part of India they are not strictly observed. Whatever the case may be, all important festivals are celebrated throughout India with gaiety, enthusiasm and religious fervour. It cannot be however said that there is a uniformity in the manner of celebrating festivals. The differences are apparent, which are due to the regional variations in customs, manners and traditions. They show the habits, customs, practices and ways of life of people belonging to different regions.

The Hindu festivals in our country are classified into three broad groups. The first group comprises festivals like Dassera and Deepavali. They are observed throughout the country more or less in a similar manner without any differences. Prof. M. N. Srinivas calls them as "All India Sanscritic Hinduism" since they have uniformity in the observance. The second group consists of Vratas such as Varalakshmi vratam, Satyanarayana vratam and Mangala Gowri vratam etc. The third group includes Jataras which are localised in character. They are celebrated in adoring and propitiating the village deities. They have some legal and religious significance. Despite the categorisation, the Hindus regard the festivals, vratas and jataras as common to all. Nevertheless, the jataras associated with the rural areas differ widely in the way of their celebrations from one area to the other.

Again some festivals are Vedic in nature some Sanscritic and others Tantric or Puranic Cult in nature or in their origin and development. The Smritis say that on these festival days people are expected to observe certain dharmas like charity, mercy, patience and observe certain taboos like sexual intercourse.

The Hindu working women observe various festivals with a view to obtain prosperity and security for the entire caste or community as family. They observe fasts, worship various Gods and Goddesses and after the ceremonial rites they enjoy grand feasts.

The following are some of the important periodic festivals celebrated by the Hindu working women in Tirupati. Apart from these main festivals, the Hindu working women also worship some of the local deities such as Gangamma, Vesha-lamma and Mutyalamma.

Sankranti

Sankrati is a festival celebrated in the month of January (in Pushyamasa of Hindu month) every year. On this day, the Sun's entry into the Capricon of the Zodiac is taken into account. It is also popularly known as Pedda Panduga. From this day onwards Uttarayana commences. It is considered very important. This festival is mainly associated with the worship of souls of the departed ancestors. Sankranti festival lasts for three days. Bhogi is observed on the first day, Makara Sankranti or Peddapanduga and Kanuma Panduga on the second and the third days respectively.

On the first day of Bhogi, before sunrise the house is cleaned thoroughly and a huge bonafire is lit in front of the house in which all old and useless things are thrown and burnt.

The cowdung balls with yellow pumpkin flowers called as 'Gobbillu' are placed at the entrance of house and it is beautifully decorated with Rangoli and mango leaves. The householders invite their sons-in law, daughters and their children for the festival and present them with new clothes and other gifts.

Bhogi means the festival of enjoyment and probably has its origin in the beginning of the harvest. In addition to this, the dairy products are also available in abundance. Hence, the people are happy and cheerful. According to Hindu Sastras the period of eight hours as the sun enters into capricon is considered very auspicious and sacred. Therefore, the orthodox people worship the souls of the departed and offer shradda in order to appease them. All the Hindus eagerly look forward to the punyakala to perform various religious rituals.

The second day is called 'Sankranti' or 'Pedda Panduga' (in Telugu). It is believed that the sun seated in his luminous chariot is drawn by seven respondent steeds, journeys northwards from southwards (Uttarayana) on this day. It is an auspihious day not only to the living but also to the dead. On this day, pongal is cooked in a pot with rice, dhal, milk, sugar or jaggery and it is kept in the open as it is meant to be the offering to the sun. On this day the family members worship the household deities and observe fastings.

The third day is observed as Kanuma Panduga. It is a festival of cows. The cow is held in high esteem by Hindus. Hindus worship cows. According to Dharma Sastras, cow is regarded as sacred animal. This day is characterised by "Gopuja". It is an important festival for agriculturists. They worship cattle, especially, cows and the bulls are decorated with flowers, bells and leather ornaments. By performing this festival the Hindus feel assured of their cattle's health and also feel as if they have done their duty towards the cattle with an overwhelming sense of gratification.

All Hindu working women (271 respondents) belonging to all castes observe Sankranti with great rejoicing and religious fervour.

Maha Sivaratri

There are several Itihasas regarding Maha Sivaratri festival. All Hindu working women respondents observe this festival in Tirupati in order to appease Lord Siva in the month of Magha. The importance of this festival is that the day is considered equivalent to the entire month. Prior to the festival day, the Hindus clean their houses in a traditional manner. On the festival day early in the morning, all the members of family wake up and take purificatory bath. The elders of the family observe fasting and worship the deity in the evening. Women go to the Siva temples and worship Siva Lingam with bilva leaves. They offer coconuts, plantains, and a preparation of gram/rice and jaggery. After returning home with food offering, they eat but their food consists of boiled vegetables and some sweet dishes. Generally, most of the people consider it desirable to keep awake for the whole night. For the purpose a programme like Harikatha and special movies are arranged by a group of people. Here also the Hindu working women actively participate and spend their time with joy and happiness.

The twice-born castes like Brahmins and Kshatriyas observe this festival with great religious fervour. The other caste working women also equally observe the festival, but with less pomp and gaiety. However, all the 271 Hindu working women recognise the religious significance of the day.

Ganesh Chaturthi

Ganesh Chaturthi or Vinayaka Chaviti is celebrated on the fourth day in the Hindu month of Bhadrapada. It is important to all Hindus throughout the country. The presiding deity of this festival is Lord Ganesha, the son of Lord Siva. He is looked upon as having assumed forms of Siddhi. People buy the specially prepared idols of Ganesh from the shops. The idols are placed in central pantheon part of the house. First, they clean the house and decorate it in traditional and ritual manner. They spread some leaves and rice on them and cover with a new cloth. A sacred thread is put on the idol. The idol is then marked with vermillion and turmeric powder. There are some special features for observing this festival. First the occupational castes worship their material things, the business people worship their account books and the children their text books. Second, all Hindus believe that seeing the moon on this festival day without worshipping God is inauspicious and not sacred. Further, the Hindus believe that their goals will be achieved without any obstacies. All the Hindu woıking women celebrate the festival on a grand scale with pomp and joy. They perform this festival every year in order to maintain peace and harmony both in the family and in the work spot. There is no other festival, perhaps in the country as a whole, which is so widespread and so popularly celebrated. The Hindu Sastras lay down that before commencing any Karma, the worship of Ganesh should first be observed.

All the 271 Hindu working women observe this festival in accordance with ihe strict observance of rituals.

Diwal

The word 'Diwali' is a corruption of the Sanskrit word 'Deepavali' means 'Cluster of lights'. This is the new year day of the Hindus who follow the Vikram era. The festival falls in October-November i.e., in the Hindu month of Ashvayuja. Hindus celebrate this festival for a period of two days. It is one of the important festivals for Hindus throughout the country. Particularly for children it is an important festival, as during the celebration, they burn variety of crackers with great fun, enthusiasm and joy.

Different legends are narrated to account for its origin. One is that King Vikramaditya was crowned on this day. Another legend tells that Bali was deprived of his Kingdom by Vishnu. Yet another legend tells that Lord Vishnu, the protector killed Narakasura (A demon of filth) accompanied by Satyabhama on this day. Hence, people call this festival as "Naraka Chaturdasi".

On the first day, all Hindus wake up early in the morning and have their purificatory bath and wear new clothes. All men, women and children look colourful in their dress. The Hindu working women of higher castes take lighted wicks in a plate and wave them before their husbands and offer arati in the early hours. Later, they worship the family deities and offer them the cooked food. On the same day evening, every house shines brilliantly with earthen lamps. They worship the Lakshmi, the Goddess of wealth, the consort of Lord Vishnu.

The second day is called "Deepavali". In the evening rows of earthern lamps and candles are arranged in each house. Some of the Hindu working women perform 'Nomulu' on this day. It is their traditional practice. They perform these 'Nomulu' for the welfare of the family. On both days sweets are prepared and distributed to friends.

All the 271 Hindu working women respondents observe the festival with pomp and show, gaiety and religious favour.

Desara

This festival takes place as the culmination of Navaratri (Nine nights) celebrations. It is observed during the first half of the month of Ashvayuja (September-October) and it lasts for nine days. The festival is devoted to the worship of Adi Sakti. During the festival of Saraswati, the Goddess of knowledge is worshipped from the day when the moon transits over the Moola Constellation to the day of the Sravana star.

All the three principal Goddesses of the pantheon are worshipped during Navaratri—Durga or Adi sakti, the Goddess of power and energy during the first three days, Lakshmi, the Goddess of wealth the next three days and Saraswati, the Goddess of knowledge in the last three days.

This festival is observed by all Hindu working women in special honour of Durga, the Goddess of Hindu pantheon i.e. Adi Sakti. Particularly Brahmins, Vysyas and Viswa Brahmins celebrate it with grandeur and pomp. They arrange "Bommala

Koluvu" (display of variety of dolls) on these days.

Sree Rama Navami

This festival is observed in honour of the incarnation of Lord Rama, which comes on the ninth day of the first half of the month of Chaitra (March—April). It lasts for one day. The people regard this day as very sacred and observe fasts and perform bhajans. On this day, the Ramayana, one of the greatest Hindu scriptures is read in private houses and temples.

The Narada Purana states that on this auspicious day one should observe fasting and offer food or clothes to the Brahmins, as by doing so one will obtain both religious merit and salvation. Some families distribute food to the poor.

The Hindu working women worship the idol of Rama in their respective houses and also in temples by offering coconuts, flowers and fruits. All the 271 Hindu working women celebrate this festival though with less pomp and show. It is learnt that 95 respondents belonging to Brahmin, Vysya and Viswa Brahmin, Vysya and Viswa Brahmins observe fasting on this festival day.

Krishna Jayanti

It is observed on the eighth day of Shravana (August-September). It is believed on this auspicious and sacred day Lord Krishna is said to have been born. It is, however, confined to a limited number of families. The main ritual ceremony takes place at mid-night. All Hindus believe that at this hour, Lord Sri Krishna was born as an incarnation of Lord Vishnu, one of the Trinities. A sweet dish is prepared and distributed to those who attend the mid-night worship. Some women observe fasting the next day in order to pay their homage to Lord Krishna.

Though all the 271 Hindu working women attach due religious significance to this festival, they do not celebrate it unlike the North Indians with great jubiliation and joy.

Nagula Chaviti

Nagula Chaviti is an important festival held on the fifth day of the month of Kartika. It is a festival of Cobra. People especially women worship the King Cobra. The worship of Naga is very ancient in this country. On this day, women go to the nearest ant-heap which is a favourite abode of the King Cobra with milk, flowers and a special dish prepared with gingelly seeds, rice, jaggery called as "Chalimidi". They pour milk into the ant-heap. All Hindu working women especially the lower castes firmly believe that by performing this puja they will be free from dangerous diseases and barreness. The serpants are regarded as Devatas.

Ugadi

It comes in the month of Chaitra (March-April) and is observed by all communities. It denotes the beginning of the Telugu New Year. The beginning of the month calculated on the basis of the astro-mathematical science called as "Ugadi". There is a great variation on the reckoning of time (Kala) from state to state in our country. In the Southern States, the days and months are generally calculated from the sun's entry into Zodaical signs, Aries, etc. In Northern States Bhruhaspati system is in vogue and as such, the beginning of the new year differs. But for the performance of all rituals associated with Karma Kanda, the Lunar months are very important and auspicious for all Hindus, throughout the country.

The main features of the day are regarding the new almanac and bearing the forecast of the events of the new year. Early in the morning the old and the young of both sexes wake up and take oil bath and wear new clothes. Some give alms to the poor and worship God. Women prepare a special dish with new tamarind, jaggery, mango, sugarcane, and neem flowers. This special dish is called as "Ugadi Pachchadi". Only after tasting this, they take other special dishes prepared on the occasion. The Hindu working women believe that the happenings of this day will forebode and colour the entire year ahead. All the Hindu respondents celebrate it with the accompanyment of religious sentiment and pleasure.

All Muslim working women, and 21 Christian working women observe and celebrate their respective festivals such as Ramzan, Mhakrid, Muharram, Shabe Sharat and Meelad Nabi with great enthusiasm and joy, pomp and show, religious fevour and happinsss.

Jataras

The deities belonging to the little traditional level are called as "Gramadevatalu". Tne worship of these daities varies from region. People believe that these deities protect the village from all calamities and evils. It is one of the important characteristic features of the village deities in the State of Andhra Pradesh. The people, both educated and uneducated, worship and propitiate them, celebrate Jataras on appropriate occasions and offer them sacrifices in order to protect them from various diseases like cholera and small pox. People of all types believe that it is very essential to worship these local deities for general welfare.

The popular female deities in the region of Tirupati are Gangamma, Poleramma, Mutyalamma and Veshalamma.

Ganga Jatara

Ganga Jatara is the local festival celebrated by all Hindu castes including working women. This is the annual occasion got up in reverence to a local Goddess popularly known as Gangamma. The festival commences on the fourth Tuesday in the month of Chaitra (March-April).

The performance of this Jatara is confined only to some areas of Rayalaseema region in Andhra Pradesh. The main feature of this ceremony is offering of goats, sheep and he-buffaloes to the village deity Gangamma. The blood of the animal is sprinkled in front of the Goddess. People believe that Gangamma will protect the villagers from the invasion of witches, devils and also fetch rains. Lower caste people and some other high caste people appear in different apparels

(Veshamulu in Telugu). On the first day, they appear in white, on the second day in red (Kumkuma Veshamu) and the third day in black.

Women cook 'Pongal' (with rice, dhal and jaggery) by the side of the temple, later it is offered to the deity and then distributed to others. The Goddess is believed to be pleased with all this and does something good to crops and people. It is ascertained that not all Hindu caste working women observe this Jatara. Baring Brahmins the other caste working women observe this Jatara by visiting the temple located in the heart of the town. Especially, it is popular among the low caste people.

Table 4

Belief in Celebrating Festivals Religion-wise

Religion of the respondents	*Belief in celebrating festivals* Yes	No	*Total*
Hinduism	246	25	271
	(90.8)	(9.2)	(90.3)
Islam	8	—	8
	(100.0)		(2.7)
Christianity	21	—	21
	(100.0)		(7.0)
Total	275	25	300
	(91.7)	(8.3)	

As regards belief in celebrating festivals it is clear from the Table 4 that a greater percentage of the respondents (90.8 per cent) confessed positively, while a negligible percentage, that is 9.2 per cent, responded negatively. Despite their non-belief, working women however take part in celebrating festivals partly out of compulsions from the members of family and partly imposing traditions. There respondents belonged to higher strata of the society. On the other hand, all the 21 Christian respondents and 8 Muslim respondents responded favourably. They all take part in their respective community festivals with all joy and religiosity.

Education-wise, (see Table 5), it is seen that among the believers, 57.7 per cent had post-graduate and professional qualifications, while, 22.8 per cent were graduates. Whereas among the non-believers, of the 25 respondents, 17 (68.0 per cent) were post-graduates and professionals and the remaining 8 (3.20 per cent) possessed collegiate education. It is clear from this analysis that education had its little influence on the believers. Despite their having higher educational qualifications, working women have not broken and parted with their belief in celebrating their community festivals. In this respect, they were traditionally–bound. What may be noted here is that the pomp and show with which the Hindus used to celebrate festivals has been slackened.

In our further analysis the income variable was taken to assess its influence on the respondents' belief in celebrating festivals. A wide variation could be seen in respect of respondents' income. However, the data (in Table 6) shows that despite variations in income, their belief in celebrating festivals was unaffected and unchanged. This fact is evident from the data which points out that 77.7 per cent of the total 246 Hindu believers had possessed income between Rs. 500 and Rs. 1500 at the time of assessment. While 19.1 per cent, 7.3 per cent and 0.8 per cent could be seen in the income groups, Rs. 1001-2000, Rs. 2001-2500 and Rs. 2501-3000 respectively.

Visiting Places of Worship on Festival Days

It is a customary duty that people belonging to different religions visit their respective places of worship during festival days. This custom was however not strictly adhered and followed by the respondents as revealed in the study.

Interestingly, there were visitors non-visitors and occasional visitors. Of the total 300 respondents, 47 per cent of the Hindu and all Christian respondents representing 7.0 per cent were regular visitors to their respective places of worship (see Table 7). In contrest, 18.3 per cent of the Hindu and all the Muslim respondents representing 2.7 per cent in the total sample never visited their respective places of worship. These

Table 5

Belief in Celebrating Festivals Education-wise

Belief in forms of God	*Religion of the respondents*	*Educational Level of the respondents*				*Total*
		Upto primary educa-tion	*Secondary education/ Matric/ Intermediate*	*Graduation and technical*	*Post-Graduation and Professional*	
Yes	Hinduism	10 (4.1)	38 (15.4)	56 (22.8)	142 (57.7)	256 (82.0)
	Islam	—	3 (37.5)	2 (25.0)	3 (37.5)	8 (2.7)
	Christianity	1 (4.8)	4 (19.0)	6 (28.6)	10 (47,6)	21 (7.0)
No	Hinduism	—	—	8 (32.0)	17 (68.0)	25 (8.3)
	Islam	—	—	—	—	—
	Christianity	—	—	—	—	—
Total		11 (3.7)	45 (15.0)	72 (24.0)	172 (57.3)	300

Table 6

Belief in Celebrating Festivals – Income Group Wise

Belief in forms of God	*Religion of the respondents*	*Income Groups of the Respondents (per month in Rupees)* 500-1000	1001-1500	1501-2000	2001-2500	2501-3000	*Total*
Yes	Hinduism	112 (45.5)	67 (27.2)	47 (19.1)	18 (7.3)	2 (0.8)	246 (82.0)
	Islam	6 (75.0)	—	1 (12.5)	—	1 (12.5)	8 (8.0)
	Christianity	8 (38.1)	10 (47.6)	1 (4.8)	1 (4.8)	1 (4.8)	21 (2.7)
No	Hinduism	—	—	6 (24.0)	8 (32.0)	11 (44.0)	25 (8.3)
	Islam	—	—	—	—	—	—
	Christianity	—	—	—	—	—	—
Total		126 (42.0)	77 (25.7)	55 (18.3)	27 (9.0)	15 (5.0)	300

Table 7

Number of Respondents Visiting Places of Worship on Festival Days—Age Group Wise

Visiting places of worship on festival days	*Religion of the respondents*	*Age Groups of the respondents (in years)* 15-20	21-30	31-40	41-50	51 & above	*Total*
Yes	Hinduism	—	63 (44.7)	52 (36.9)	20 (14.2)	6 (4.3)	141 (47.0)
	Islam	—	—	—	—	—	—
	Christianity	—	10 (47.6)	9 (42.9)	1 (4.6)	1 (4.8)	21 (7.0)
No	Hinduism	1 (1.8)	14 (25.5)	23 (41.8)	6 (10.9)	11 (20.0)	55 (18.3)
	Islam	—	3 (37.5)	3 (37.5)	1 (12.5)	1 (12.5)	8 (2.7)
	Christianity	—	—	—	—	—	—
Occassionaly	Hinduism	—	35 (46.7)	20 (26.7)	10 (13.3)	10 (13.3)	75 (25.0)
	Islam	—	—	—	—	—	—
	Christianity	—	—	—	—	—	—
Total	...	1 (0.3)	125 (41 7)	107 (35.7)	38 (12.7)	29 (9.7)	300

Table 8

Visiting Places of Worship on Festival Days—Education-wise

Visiting places of worship on festival days	*Religion of the respondents*	*Educational Level of the respondent*				
		Upto primary education	*Secondary education/ Matric/ Intermediate*	*Graduation and technical*	*Post-Graduation and professional*	*Total*
Yes	Hinduism	10 (7.1)	38 (27.0)	30 (21.3)	63 (44.7)	141 (47.0)
	Islam	—	—	—	—	—
	Christianity	1 (4.8)	4 (19.0)	6 (28.6)	10 (47.6)	21 (7.0)
No	Hinduism	—	—	14 (25.5)	41 (74.5)	55 (18.3)

	Islam	—	3 (37.5)	2 (25.0)	3 (37.5)	8 (2.7)
	Christianity	—	—	—	—	—
Occasionaly	Hinduism	—	—	20 (26.7)	55 (73.3)	75 (25.0)
	Islam	—	—	—	—	—
	Christianity	—	—	—	—	—
Total		11 (3.7)	45 (15.0)	72 (24.0)	172 (57.3)	300

respondents were however praying and worshipping in their respective houses. Among the occasional visitors 75.2 per cent belonged to the Hindu community.

On further analysis, it may be seen that age had little influence among the visitors. Despite wide variations in the age, the respondents were visiting their places of worship. This could be seen in the Table 7 that of the 141 Hindu visitors a higher percentage (81.6 per cent) belonged to 21 and 40 years. In the case of occasional visitors, 46.7 per cent were found in the age group of 21-30 years and only 15.3 per cent in 61 and above. Whereas among non-visitors, out of 55 Hindu respondents, 41.8 per cent belonged to the age group of 31-40 years and only one respondent could be seen in 18-20 years.

Relationship of education with the visiting places of worship during festivals is shown in Table 8. (p. 103). Analysis of data as per the level of education shows that among the Hindu visitors, significantly a high percentage of the respondents had higher educational qualification. That is, 66.0 per cent were post-graduates, professionals and graduates. Thus, education had little influence on the visitors. In sharp contrast to this, of the total 58 Hindu non-visitors, 73.3 per cent were post-graduates and 26.7 per cent graduates. In their case, education seemed to have some influence and negatively affected their visiting to the temples.

Among the visitors, education and their visiting to temples were positively related. Whereas among the non-visitors, it was negatively related. Though education has influenced both negatively and positively, the fact may be noted that the working women had firm faith in the existence of God, and it was unaffected and unaltered.

Vratas

According to Vedas 'Vrata' means to undertake a religious observance. Vratas may be described as days of fasting and prayer. Brahmin householders, wholly devoted to a religious life, usually observe all the Vratas prescribed by the religious texts. Women are very scrupulous in the observance of Vratas and spend such days in fasting, praying and performing the prescribed pujas. The most characteristic feature of the Vrata is complete fasting or absenting oneself from cooked food.

Both married and unmarried working women performed Vratas to procure the good health of their children, good husbands, saubhagya, prosperity, happiness and the removal of spirits and evils. In short, all conceivable temporal bliss can be attained. The attainment of both 'Bhakti' and 'Mukti' are associated with the performance of these Vratas.

Our study revealed that Vratas were popular among the forward caste working women. Out of 271 Hindu respondents, 38.7 per cent observed various Vratas like Varalakshmi Vratam, Satyanarayana Vratam, Gowri Vratam and Kedareswara Vratam. These respondents belonged to upper castes, Brahmins (63), Kshatriyas (15), Vysyas (10), Balijas (10), Kammas (16) and Maharashtra Brahmins (2). Brahmin respondents celebrated all Vratas, while other caste respondents observed one or two Vratas, namely, Satyanarayana and Varalakshmi Vratams. They performed these Vratas for the benefit of the whole family. Performing Vratas is a traditional practice. If any one fails to perform vratas, it is said that one may have to suffer from various afflictions.

Varalakshmi Vratam

Varalakshmi Vratam is celebrated on the last Friday of the bright fortnight in the month of "Ashada" corresponding to the English month July-August. Both married and unmarried women are eligible to perform this Vrata. It is a Vrata to propitiate the Goddess Lakshmi, the consort of Vishnu, one of the Hindu Trinity. It is observed by women invoking the blessings of Lakshmi for good health, welfare and prosperity of the family.

Satyanarayana Vratam

It is sacred and performed in adoration of Lord Vishnu not on a fixed day of the calender but on any convenient day. Both husband and wife perform this Vrata. It is somewhat

Table 9
Number of Respondents Performing Vratas According to Educational Level

Performing Vratas	*Religion of the Respondents*	*Educational Level of the respondents*				*Total*
		Upto primary education	*Secondary education/ Matric/Intermediate*	*Graduation and technical*	*Post-Graduation and professional*	
Yes	Hinduism	10 (8.6)	25 (12.6)	40 (34.5)	41 (35.3)	116 (38.7)
	Islam	—	—	—	—	—
	Christianity	—	—	—	—	—
Don't perform	Hinduism	—	13 (8.4)	24 (15.5)	118 (76.1)	155 (51.7)
	Islam	—	3 (37.5)	2 (25.0)	3 (37.5)	8 (2.7)
	Christianity	1 (4.8)	4 (19.0)	6 (28.6)	10 (47.6)	21 (7.0)
Total		11 (3.7)	45 (15.0)	72 (24.0)	172 (57.3)	300

expensive and it involves inviting a large number of friends and relatives. It is believed that whoever performs this Vrata with a real devotion and hears the sacred stories of Vishnu will get the grace of Lord Satyanarayana.

Relationship of education variable with observing Vratas by the working women is shown in Table 9. In the study it was found that all Christian and Muslim respondents have not known any Vratas of their religion. Only Hindus perform Vratas. Out of a total of 300 respondents, 116 (38.7 per cent) performed Vratas and 155 (51.7 per cent) did not. The percentage of non-observers is higher than that of the observers. Education-wise, out of 116 Hindu respondents, 35.3 per cent were post-graduates and 34.5 per cent graduates. Whereas in the case of non-performers a big variation could be seen. 118 Hindu respondents (76.1 per cent) out of 155 were post-graduates and professionals. So, it is proved that education had significant influence upon performing Vratas by the Hindu working women.

Fasting

Fasting is a part of religious life. All religions including Christianity and Islam emphasise the necessity of fasting as a discipline and preparation for penitence. Fasting literally means total abstinence from food and drink, but generally it means light diet restricted in quantity and also as regards the nature of the articles taken. Muslim working women observe fasting during the month of Ramzan while Christian working women during Easter. Hindu working women however observe fasting on a number of occasions. Observing fasting by the respondents is shown in Table 10. The data shows that all Muslim women observed fasting since their religion insisted on purification of the body. In the case of Christians, out of 21, 12 observed fasting on some occasions while 9 did not.

The relationship between education and observing fasting has been studied. A significant relationship could be seen. Of 127 Hindu observers, 46.4 per cent were post graduates followed by 29.9 per cent who had secondary and Intermediate education. All the 10 primary literates observed fasting on some

Table 10

Number of Respondents Observing Fasting-Education Wise

Performing Vratas	*Religion of the respondents*	*Eaucational Level of the respondent*				*Total*
		Upto primary education	*Secondary education/ Matric/ Intermediate*	*Graduation and technical*	*Post-Graduation and professional*	
Occasionaly	Hinduism	10 (7.9)	38 (29.9)	20 (15.7)	59 (46.4)	127 (42.3)
	Islam	—	3 (37.5)	2 (25.0)	3 (37.5)	8 (2.7)
	Christianity	1	4	3	4	12
Never	Hinduism	—	—	44 (30.5)	100 (69.4)	144 (43.0)
	Islam	—	—	—	—	—
	Christianity	—	—	3 (33.3)	6 (66.7)	9 (3.0)
Total		11 (3.7)	45 (15.0)	72 (24.0)	172 (57.3)	300

occasions. In sharp contrast, out of 144 Hindu respondents who did not observe fasting 69.4 per cent were post-graduates and 30.5 per cent graduates. From this analysis, it may be inferred that the working women who did not observe fasting are more than the working women who observed it. The former group specified the reasons such as performing dual role both at home and outside, preoccupation with number of works, attitudinal changes and education. All these contributed significantly to the change in their perception regarding fasting.

Table 11

The Reasons for Fasting

Religion of the respondents	*Reasons for keeping fasting*			*Total*
	For the longivity of the husband	*Purification of the body*	*Traditional practice*	
Hindusim	74 (27.30%)	80 (29.52%)	117 (43.17%)	271
Islam	—	8 (100.0%)	—	8
Christianity	—	21 (100%)	—	21
Total	74 (24.6%)	109 (36.3%)	117 (39.0%)	300

In our study the respondents observing fasting furnished three important reasons. They are for longivity of the husband, purification of the body and perpetuatiug traditional practice.

The Table 11 presents the reasons for fasting. Out of 271 Hindu respondents, 74 (27.30 per cent) observed fasting for the longivity of their husbands, 82 (29.52 per cent) for purification of the body and 117 (43.17 per cent) for perpetuating traditional practice. All 8 Muslim and 21 Christian respondents observed fasting for purification of the body. It may be thus concluded that though the percentage of working women observing fasting is a littie high, it has not affected significant percentage of working women. The practice of observing fasting is still in vogue despite the level of education and occupation.

Praying

In all religions prayer is common to make a vow in which the individual promises to carry out a certain kind of behaviour such as breaking the coconut, offering fruit and flowers to the diety, going on a pilgrimage or building a temple if the dieties grant a particular wish. Relationship between education and praying is presented in Table-12.

Analysis of the data shows significant positive and negative relationship. It may be seen that all 8 Muslims and 21 Christians prayed to God regularly. In their case education had very little influence. Their respective religions strongly demand them to pray and worship God regularly. Usually, Muslims offer prayers on Fridays and Christians on Sundays. On the contrary, in the case of Hindus, 132 working women, that is about 44 per cent, prayed to God regularly and 139 working women, that is nearly 46.8 per cent, occasionally. Among those praying occasionally, 71.2 per cent were post-graduates and 28.8 per cent graduates. The reason for such disparity is quite obvious. Hinduism unlike other religions does not insist upon the believers to pray to God regularly. It is quite flexible. However, this has not maned their faith in God and it is unchanged. All the respondents firmly believed in God. Since working women were preoccupied with their work and since they were wanted in discharging many roles, they could find little time at their disposal to pray to God. Interestingly, those praying occasionally among Hindus were more than those praying regularly. Nevertheless, they were, as they confessed staunch believers in the existence of God.

Belief in Magic

Magic is a term used for a wide range of phenomena, from the elaborate ritual beliefs and practices that are at the core of many religious systems, to acts of conjuring for entertainment used. In the former sense, magic is a social and

Table 12
Praying of God—Education wise

Praying to God	*Religion of the respondents*	*Educational Level of the respondents*				*Total*
		Upto primary education	*Secondary education/ Matric/ Intermediate*	*Graduation and technical*	*Post-Graduation and professional*	
Regularly	Hinduism	10 (7.6)	38 (21.8)	24 (18.2)	60 (45.5)	132 (44.0)
	Islam	—	3 (37.5)	2 (25.0)	3 (37.5)	8 (2.7)
	Christianity	1 (4.7)	4 (19.0)	6 (28.6)	10 (47.6)	21 (7.0)
Occasionally	Hinduism	—	—	40 (28.8)	99 (71.2)	139 (46.3)
	Islam	—	—	—	—	—
	Christianity	— (4.8)	— (19.0)	— (28.6)	— (47.6)	— (7.0)
Total		11 (3.7)	45 (15.0)	72 (24.0)	172 (57.3)	300

cultural phenomenon found in all places and at all periods with varying degrees of importance. It is a kind of pseudo science by which an early man attempted to manipulate nature. It refers to ritual performance or activity that is thought to lead to the influencing of human or natural events by an external and impersonal mystical force beyond the ordinary human sphere. The performance involves the use of objects or the recitation of spells or both by the magicians.

Durkeim, Emile observes that magic has no place of worship or group. Practitioners of magic carry out their functions on an individual basis much like a doctor treating patients. Religion is on the other hand purely communal and universal. It is not directed at a single individual but carried out for the benefit of the whole community. It is more universal than magic which is localised and purely individualistic in character.

The study (Table-13) reveals the fact that all 21 Christians and 8 Muslims did not believe in magic. In these two faiths, magic has no religious and social sanction. It too had no sanction among the Hindus respondents. An overwhelming percentage (98.4 per cent) of them did not believe in magic. Education-wise, 159 Hindu respondents (59.8 per cent) were post-graduates and professionals and 24.1 per cent graduates, while a negligible 2.6 per cent belonged to the category of secondary and primary education. Only 5 respondents of them, 3 belonging to primary education and 2 to secondary education, expressed their belief in magic It may be concluded that majority of working women did dot believe in magic. Here, education has significant positive relationship.

Belief in Fate

Work action done in a former existence and leading to inevitable results in the present is called fate. The Sanskritic language has various equivalents for the word fate such as Kala (time) and Vidhi (destiny). The accomplishment of an object is divided between fate and exertion. Of these, the fate is the manifestation of one's acts in former life. Some expect

Table 13
Belief in Magic-Education Wise

Belief in Magic	*Religion of the respondents*	*Upto primary education*	*Secondary education/ Matric/ Intermediate*	*Graduation and technical*	*Post Graduation and prefessional*	*Total*
		Educational Level of the respondents				
Belief	**Hinduism**	3 (60.0)	2 (40.0)	—	—	5 (1.7)
	Islam	—	—	—	—	—
	Christianity	—	—	—	—	—
Disbelief	**Hinduism**	7 (2.6)	36 (13.5)	64 (24.1)	159 (39.8)	266 (88.7)
	Islam	—	3 (37.5)	2 (12.5)	3 (37.5)	8 (2.7)
	Christianity	1 (4.8)	4 (19.0)	6 (28.6)	10 (47.6)	21 (7.0)
Total		11 (3.7)	45 (15.0)	72 (24.0)	172 (57.3)	300

success from fate, some from accident. Some from the lapse of time and some from effort. Men of genius believe in the efficacy of the combination of all these. Fate binds a man with iron cords and drags him upwards to the highest rank or downward to the depths of misery. Table 14 presents the belief and disbelief of the 300 working women in respect of fate.

It may be seen that all Christians and Muslims believed in Fate, while in the case of Hindu respondents they were mostly divided. Out of 300 working women an overwhelming majority of 220 Hindu respondents believed in fate. Their percentage is 73.3. Of them 60 per cent were post-graduates and professional and 18.2 percent graduates. 17.3 per cent and 4.5 per cent of the respondents belonged to secondary and primary education respectively. Fairly an insignificant percentage, 17 per cent (that is 51 respondents), expressed no belief in fate, of them 27 (52.9 per cent) were post-graduates and 24 (47.1 per cent) graduates. It may be drawn from the data that education has very little influence on working women in their belief and disbelief in fate.

Belief in Fortune Telling

Table 15 gives us a picture of the belief and disbelief of 300 working women in fortune telling. Here, education has tremendous influence on them. Out of 300 respondents, a higher percentage of Hindus (79 per cent) and 2 per cent of Christians did not believe in fortune telling. While 34 Hindus (11.3 per cent) 8 Muslims (27 per cent) and 15 Christians (5 per cent) believed in fortune telling.

Education-wise, in respect of disbelief, out of 237 Hindus respondents, 159 (69 per cent) were found as postgraduates, 64 (27 per cent) graduates and the remaining 14 (5.9 per cent) possessed secondary and intermediate education. So, in the case of fortune telling majority of respondents, that is out of 300 working women, 243 did not believe in it. Their total percentage is 81.0. As the analysis shows, education has a greater impact on this particuiar religious belief.

Belief in Good and Evil Omens

Omens are in fact the indicators of probable success or

Table 14
Belief in Fate—Education Wise

Belief in fate	*Religion of the respondents*	*Educational Level of the respondents*				
		Upto primary education	*Secondary education/ Matric/ Intermediate*	*Graduation and technical*	*Post-Graduation and professional*	*Total*
Belief	**Hinduism**	10 (4·5)	38 (17.3)	40 (18.2)	132 (60.0)	220 (73.3)
	Islam	—	3 (37.5)	2 (12.5)	3 (37.5)	8 (2.7)
	Christianity	1 (4.8)	4 (19.0)	6 (28.6)	10 (47.6)	21 (7.0)
Disbelief	**Hinduism**	—	—	24 (47.1)	27 (52 9)	51 (17·0)
	Islam	—	—	—	—	—
	Christianity	—	—	—	—	—
Total		11 (3.7)	45 (15.0)	72 (24.0)	172 (57.3)	300

Table 15

Belief in Fortune Telling—Education-wise

Belief in fortune telling	*Religion of the respondents*	*Educational Level of the respondents* — *Upto primary education*	*Secondary education/ Matric/ Intermediate*	*Graduation and technical*	*Post-Graduation and professional*	*Total*
Belief	Hinduism	10 (29.4)	25 (70.6)	—	—	34 (11.3)
	Islam	—	3 (37.5)	2 (25.0)	3 (37.5)	8 (2.7)
	Christianity	1 (6.7)	4 (26.7)	4 (26.6)	6 (40.0)	15 (5.0)
Disbelief	Hinduism	—	14 (5.9)	64 (27.0)	159 (67.0)	237 (79.0)
	Islam	—	—	—	—	—
	Christianity	—	—	2 (33.3)	4 (66.7)	6 (2.0)
Total		11 (3.7)	45 (15.0)	72 (24.1)	172 (57.3)	300

failure of a particular venture. It is believed that if a good omen occurs that task will be accomplished. If a bad omen occurs the success is doubtful.

It may be seen in the Table 16 that out of 300 respondents 194 Hindus (64.7 per cent), 8 Muslims (2.7 per cent) and 13 Christians (4.3 per cent) believed in omens. Whereas 77 Hindus (25.7 per cent) and 8 Christians (2.7 per cent) did not believe in them. Education has no great impact on working women in this particular belief. Out of 194 Hindus believers, significantly a high percentage were post-graduates (50.5 per cent) and graduates (24.7 per cent) Similarly, out of 77 Hindu non-believers, 61 79.2 per cent) were post-graduates, followed by 16 (20.8 per cent) graduates. Despite their education, majority of working women had strong belief in omens.

Conclusion

In conclusion, the festivals in Tirupati are observed on each occasion with special significance. They give an idea about the devotional and religious attitude of the people. Due to the impact of several factors such as secularisation, modernisation and the spread of education, the devotion, tradition and passion with which the festivals, Vratas and Jataras are celebrated are now slowly loosing their importance. The people's attitude and interest have also changed to a greater extent.

Certain changes due however discernible in respect of religious beliefs and disbeliefs among working women. Education was taken into account as the main variable of influencing factor. In the case of fasting, magic and fortune-telling, the impact of education upon the working women is quite revealing and positive Whereas in the case of belief in fate, the influence of education was shown as negative and not quite encouraging. This is evident from the fact that out of 300 respondents an overwhelming percentage expressed their strong belief in fate.

Whatever the changes that could be seen in respect of religious, beliefs and disbeliefs, the fact is that their internal beliefs end convictions such as their faith in the existence of

Table 16

Belief and Disbelief in Good and Evil Omens—Education Wise

Belief in good and evil omens	*Religion of the respondents*	*Educational Level of the respondents*				
		Upto primary education	*Secondary education/ Matric/ Intermediate*	*Graduation and technical*	*Post-Graduation and professional*	*Total*
Belief	Hinduism	10 (5.2)	38 (19.6)	48 (24.7)	98 (50.5)	194 (64.7)
	Islam	—	3 (37.5)	2 (26.0)	3 (37.5)	8 (2.7)
	Christianity	1 (7.7)	4 (30.8)	6 (46.2)	2 (15.4)	13 (4.3)
Disbelief	Hinduism	—	—	16 (20.8)	61 (79.2)	77 (25.7)
	Islam	—	—	—	—	—
	Christianity	—	—	—	8 (100.0)	8 (2.7)
Total		11 (3.7)	45 (15.0)	72 (24.0)	172 (57.3)	300

God could not be completely undermined and severely shaken. Their religiosity could not be questioned. They still imbibe greater spirit, inspiration enthusiasm and guidance from religion. They are down to their hearts truly religious, though certain changes could be seen in respect of observing various rituals and cumbersome procedures involved in festivals.

5

Summary and Conclusions

Religion is one of those imponderable things that cannot be assessed in quantitative terms. It is an aspect which involves beliefs, superstitions, feelings, fear, worship and attitudes of reverence. Merely by the external look of a person, one may not say whether he is religious or irreligious and if either how deeply. One who never lets slip an opportunity to publicly affirm his faith in God may be very inhuman not to say undivine in his conduct towards others. Another who repeatedly protests and says that he has no belief in God may be protesting too much. If it is hard to say how much religious an individual person is, it must be many times harder to determine the religiosity of a nation or people as a whole.

From the times of Vedic age down to the medern post-Independence of India passing through the age of the later Samhitas. Upanishads and the Epics, later Smritis and Medieval India, the role, status and position of women has not been static but has actually ranged from what is mentioned to have been one of freedom and a position of importance to the other extreme of considerable subservience. For over one thousand years India was under Muslim and Western domination. Many important segments, if not the whole fabric, of Indian society came under their influences, direct or indirect. Though significant changes did affect the traditional pattern of society, the foreign domination had not essentially altered the overwhelming majority lived in rural India.

Though during the Nineteenth century, social and religious reformers like Raja Ram Mohan Roy, Dayananda Saraswati, Eswarachandra Vidyasagar, Swami Vivekananda, Jyotiba Phuley, Mahatma Gandhi, Ramakrishna, Maha Deo Ranade and others made efforts through legal measures and educational programmes to eradicate some of the evils in Hindu society, they did not altogether change the basic tenets of Hindusim. Even today, despite the impact of certain factors such as modernisation, urbanisation, the rapid development of science and technology, the spread of education and the mass media, the basic Hindu values have not been affected and changed.

It is true that Hindu women whether working or not may have given up certain rituals and practices. But the truth is established beyond doubt that Hindu women have not abandoned their essential beliefs and faiths. Hindu tradition, bound up with domestic rituals and customs, was held together mainly by women. In fact, the cultural heritage of India was passed from generation to generation through the help of women. They were brought up in a severe and rigid tradition which made the m adhere with deliberate care to what their elders had passed one them. This provided the basis of family and community life which in turn strengthened group mores. In the modern times, the higher education facilitated them in several occupations. Today we see them having been employed as doctors, engineers, executives, typists, clerks and lecturers. Hence, they are compelled to spend their time for discharging their occupational duties. This might have led them to concentrate less time on the practice and observance of rituals, traditions and customs in their day-to-day life. Or, this must have forced them to give up certain rituals. Nonetheless, the impact of these influences could not greatly undermine their faith in traditional customs and practices, norms and values.

The study was based on Questionnaires with 300 working women which included 271 Hindus, 8 Muslims and 21

Christians. The study was made on the basis of certain conditions and limitations. First, though Christians and Muslims have been taken into account, the major emphasis was stressed upon Hindu working women. Second, all the working women belonged to Tirupati town. Third, the sample group of 271 respondents comprised Hindu women from different castes, broadly categorised into three : Forward Castes consisting of Kapu, Kamma, Brahmin, Vysya, Nair, Balija and Maharashtra Brahmin and the Backward Castes including Viswa Brahmin, Yadava, Gandla, Besta, Rajaka (Chakali), Dasari, Karanam, Odde, Jangame, Sale, Kummara, Dudekula and the Scheduled Castes i.e., Harijans. Fourth, the 300 respondents had educational qualifications ranging from primary and secondary education to graduation, post-graduation and professional courses including technical. For the purpose of understanding changes in religious practices and beliefs, education was taken as an important influencing variable. Further, for better analysis and understanding the respondents have been divided into four groups :

(1) Upto Primary Education ;
(2) Secondary/Matric/Intermediate Education ;
(3) Graduation and Technical ;
(4) Post-graduation and Professional Education ;
(5) The age of the respondents was also taken into account while assessing the changes.

They were formed between the ages of 15 and 50 and above. The age of the respondents was divided in five groups (1) 15-20; (2) 21-30; (3) 31-40; (4) 41-50; and (5) 51 and above. While studying changes in respect of belief in the forms of God, visiting places of worship, age was also considered as an important influencing factor. The sixth limitation is the income of the respondents. The income of the respondents ranged from Rs. 500 to Rs. 3,000 and above per month. The respondents have been divided into five income groups—(1) Rs. 500-1,000; (2) Rs. 1,001-1,501; (3) Rs. 1,501-2,000; (4) Rs. 2,001-2,500 and (5) 2,500-3,000. In celebrating festivals income of the respondents was also considered, The last limitation of the study is that in all changes in religious belief and ritual practices education has been mainly viewed as the most influencing factor. The occupational role in this regard has received very little attention for the reason the author strongly felt that occupation was linked with education. Since semi-literates figured in the study, it might not have been possible to take occupation into consideration. In addition, the problem arose with the categorisation of different occupations of the respondents. Hence, for these reasons, occupation was not considered as much as education.

While examining and measuring the changes in respect of religious beliefs, education has been taken as an important variable. As for instance, visiting places of worship, celebrating festivals, performing vratas, observing fasting, praying to God, belief in magic, belief in fate, belief in fortune-telling and belief in good and evil omens, educational background of the respondents has received main attention. Their occupations have not been considered, since the respondents had varied jobs and the problem was found with their categorisation. However, the income factor has been considered in the case of celebrating festivals and the age of respondents has received its due attention in respect of belief in forms of God and visiting places of worship.

Necessary information was obtained from the respondents by means of Questionnaires. Each of the respondents was given an open-ended questionnaire to fill out as fully as possible. The respondents were told that they could write as much as they wished with regard to any of the questions. Each questionnaire contained 70 questions on subjects like, social background of the respondent, belief in celebrating the samskaras, beliefs in fortune-telling, fasting, idol worship, heaven and hell, celebrations of various festivals, vratas and jataras and observance of religious rituals, practices and ceremonies.

The sample constituting 300 respondents was selected by employing at Random method. The study sought to assess the changes in their attitude towards the practice and observance of rituals and ceremonies in their day-to-day life. It tried to see and to want extent changes were effective and whether the changes were superficial or deeper and real.

The attitude of working women with regard to the value of practising and observing the rituals and ceremonies is very interesting. An analysis of the respondents of the 300 working women clearly shows that the changes were not deeper. Though they gave up some traditional beliefs and practices, they retained the essential rituals associated with various ceremonies and festivals. As for instance, in the case of first puberty ceremony, all essential rituals were followed except the presence of paternal aunt, as it was in the past, was not made compulsory. During subsequent menstruations, no seclusion was observed. The girl would simply take oil bath and attend all domestic and non-domestic work. They rarely worshipped domestic deities.

According to the respondents, there is one Supreme God, the Almighty. They recognised one God manifesting the entire universe. In this respect no difference of opinion was found among the respondents representing three religions. Nevertheless, Hindu working women believed in pantheism. They recognised and realised various Gods and Goddesses and worshipped them in their day-to-day life with reverence and fervour. Besides, they preserved the idols and images of their family deities and worshipped them on appropriate occasions. Notwithstanding the idea of one God, a few educated informants questioned the creation of universe by God. Some even gave scientific explanations for natural phenomena and creation of human beings on the earth.

Hinduism has been renewing itself from time to time. Many saints and philosophers like Ramanujacharya, Sankaracharya and Madhva during the middle ages, social and religious reformers such as Rama Krishna Paramahansa, Swami Vivekananda, Raja Ram Mohan Roy, Swami Dayananda Saraswati, Annie Besant, Bala Gangadhara Tilak, Mahadeo

Ranade, Mahatma Gandhi brought several reforms in Hinduism and gave it to the people in simplest language. These reformers sustained Hinduism against foreign invasions and made it more vigorous, authoritative, lively and lovely. In spite of all these changes, the essence of Hinduism, being the ultimate Reality i.e., changeless, eternal, ominipotent, Omniscient and omnipresent has not been distorted and nullified. The tenets of Hinduism, the non-duality of the God-head, the divinity of the soul, the unity of existence, the harmony of religions and the theory of Karma and Rebirth are unaffected and unchanged. They are still preserved with all the religious sanction and authority.

Regarding the observance of pujas and vratas, 155 out of 171 Hindu respondents did not perform them partly because they received very little cooperation and help from the members of family and partly because they discharged the dual roles both in and outside the home—the family role and the occupational role. 116 respondents observed important Vratas like Satyanarayana Vratam, Varalakshmi Vratam and Kedareswari Vratam on any auspicious day as they felt it convenient. These respondents took part while others celebrated and observed them. However, they worshipped the Hindu Gods in their homes without any specified rituals.

In respect of festivals, all Christian and Muslim respondents observed and celebrated their festivals with all gaiety and religious fervour but with less pomp and show. However, variations could be seen among Hindu working women. 25 respondents (9.2 per cent) did not participate in all festivals. 246 respondents (90.8 per cent) celebrated the major festivals such as Diwali, Vinayakachaturti, Ugadi (Telugu New Year's Day) and Sankranti for the religious significance with excitement and ecstacy. 58 respondents out of 246 celebrated minor festivals like Nagulachaviti (festival of snakes), Sri Krishna Jayanti, Sri Ramanavami, Kartikapurnima, Mahalaya amavasya and Ratha Saptami. Nonetheless, all the Hindu respondents expressed a deep feeling for the spirit of the auspicious day. They were conscious of deeper religious meaning. They had a feeling for the festivals whether they observed or not which they never lost. These women and their children deeply involved in the preparations for the festivals. The religious day for them is not a day of prayer and contemplation but a day of rejoicing. Everyone gets special food and dressed up in best. It is really a form of entertainment with song and dance. These important days were not kept strictly according to accepted customs, but the essential rituals were performed and observed by the Hindus. They visited the temples on these special days if at all possible with offerings of flowers, fruits and money.

All Hindu respondents performed the most important rites connected with the birth and growth of the child. 63 Brahmins, 14 Kahatriyas, 2 Nairs, 10 Vysyas, 1 Maharashtra Brahmin and 4 Viswa Brahmins invited a priest for the naming ceremony (namakarana). The other respondents of other communities conducted the naming ceremony without the help of the priest. All the respondents referred panchangam for christening the baby. No respondent strictly observed Anna-prasana' ceremony (giving food to the baby in the seventh month). All respondents observed the 'tonsure ceremony' in the seventh month or ninth month or eleventh month or in the third year of the baby in which case the presence of maternal uncle was not felt must.

The usual feasting associated with such ceremonies was often omitted due to the absence of caste community members or other sympathetic people. Nevertheless, simple ceremonies were performed with less expenditure, but the necessary rituals had taken place. For them, the performance of these ceremonies had meaning in and of itself. Since each caste and family placed its own particular emphasis on ceremonies, it was pointless to get outsiders involved in something which had individual meaning and was not shared by others. Since these religious ceremonies were not like major social get-togethers like marriages, it seemed out of place to give customary feasts on such occasions.

A overwhelming majority of 237 Hindu respondents out of 271 did not believe in astrological forecasts, but in fact, they inwardly believed them and they would listen to advice when given on this basis. If a trusted family astrologer tells them to observe fast on a particular day as a means of minimising effects of a bad phase, or asked them to wear a special stone or metal, they do with all sincerity and belief. All of them have horoscopes for their children. When celebrating a marriage or engagement, building a house, or moving into a new house, they do consult the Panchang and choose the day and time considered right. They do not, however, go to the extent of finding the right time and day for minor things such as travelling. This again shows that their belief in astrology was not completely dead and vanished. They still had a strong feeling of respect for it.

As regards rituals associated with marriages, all 271 Hindus respondents believed and accepted them. However, these rituals were simplified. All the marriages were celebrated with less expenditure and pomp and show. Simple feasts were arranged at the time of marriage. The celebration of a marriage on a grand scale, however, depends on the economic position of a family. The dowry is accepted. Working women of upper castes like Kapu, Kamma, Naidu and Kshatriya pay a lot of dowry. The lower caste working women pay less or more dowry depending on their economic position. Brahmins, Viswa Brahmins and Maharashtra Brahmins pay less dowry. Vysyas, however, pay dowry in the form of gold and gifts instead of cash.

All the 271 respondents had been married between the ages of twenty and thirty-five. Of them 40 respondents did not have arranged marriages. Instead they had inter-caste marriages. The inter-caste marriages of the respondents were seen between Kapu and Kamma and Balija and Brahmin and Yadava and Dudekula. 5 Christian women had married Kapu men. After marriage they converted themselves into Hindus. The majority of 226 respondents had arranged marriages.

All the respondents did not have any special feelings about the process of selection in an arranged marriage. They never interfered in their children's selection of their partners. The final decision was however left to the children. They had liberal attitude towards marriage. They believed in arranged, love-cum-arranged, inter-caste and inter-religious marriages. Despite their liberal attitude, in certain extreme cases, the respondents insisted on traditions and conventions. Whatever the liberal outlook of the respondents might be, the dowry and the type of marriage are determined by one's own economic status and position in the society.

In respect of arranged marriages, the respondents did consult horoscopes. In other types like love marriage and inter-caste and inter-religious marriages, the horoscopes were never consulted.

All the respondents performed the most important rites connected with the death and after death when necessary. All willingly performed the after-death rites for the deceased in-laws, who included not only parents-in-law but also uncles and aunts on either side of their families. This is because they did not want to deviate from traditional practices as far as the older generation was concerned. However, the after-death customs depend on the links with the extended family, where such links exist, traditional practices are adhered to. It is perhaps necessary to point out here that the lavishness with which this after-death ceremonies as also connected rituals are performed has diminished due to increased cost of living and other factors, even in the traditionally centred families.

Several rites associated with 'widowhood ceremony' have been affected with changes. The custom of the tonsure (shaving of head) of widows is absent, even among the orthodox Brahmins except in the cases of older women. As per the past traditions, a widow should be dressed in white, live as simply, unostentatiously as possible, and remain faithful to her dead husband till her own death. The more wretched and misserable she looks, the more she is respected. Society does not tolerate her attempt to live a fuller and meaningful life. She is not expected to move out freely.

As against the past traditions, a widow now wears colour saree. In certain cases, they put vermillion mark on their horehead. Out of 271 repondents, one Brahmin and two Kapus wore colour sarees, bangles, jewellery, flowers and kumkum. They moved freely in the society as they were employed. They took part in all socio-cultural and religious functions. In important religious ceremonies, they were however, not given due place, respect and honour. Widow-marriage is in vogue. Two widows from Kapu and Balija remarried.

In spite of the radical changes, the social stigmas attached to the status of a widow are such that a widow has to burn herself day in and day out for years, in the realm of taboos, prejudices and insults. She is still regarded and required to be a moving corpse. Even today, widows are expected to lead lives of ascetics.

All the Hindu, Christian and Muslim respondents believed in visiting their respective places worship. But the Hindus visited temples as and when they felt convenient. On auspicious occasions and important festival days like Sri Ramanavami, Siva Rathri and Vinayaka Chaturti, they visited temples with flowers, coconuts and fruits. Our study revealed that 141 respondents visited temples on festivals days, 75 occasionally and 55 seldom. On other days, they seldom visited the temples. Otherwise, they worshiped God and Goddesses in their homes. The lower caste women visited small temples like Gangamma Devatha, Polermma and Veshylamma for prosperity, happiness and good health. This clearly showed that though the Hindu working women rarely visited temples on all days, their faith in the existence of God was not undermined.

In respect of praying Christian and Muslim respondents prayed to God regularly. Whereas among Hindu respondents 44 per cent out of 300 prayed to God every day. 30 Brahmins and 3 Kshatriyas worshipped God offering flowers, fruits and water, chanting mantras and reading hymns from scriptures like the Bhagvad Geeta. The other 139 respondents (46.3 per cent) worshipped God occasionally by folding hands, offering arati and putting the holy mark on their forehead.

It was found that 30 Brahmins, 3 Kshatriyas and 2 Nairs have read the original scriptures, the Ramayana, the Maha Bharata and the Bhagavad Gita. The other 236 Hindu respondents have listend to the stories of scriptures as and when they were told by others. 8 Muslims and 21 Christians have read the Quaran and the Bible respectively. They, however, have read them every day as part of their prayer.

With regard to idol worship, all the 271 Hindu respondents believed in it. As contrast to them, Christian and Muslim respondents did not believe in idol worship. Among Christian respondents there were no Catholics. All of them were protestants. The Hindu respondents believed in God's reincarnations (Avataras). All 63 Brahmins, 10 Vysyas, 10 Kshatriyas and 2 Nairs firmly believed in the theory of Rebirth and Karma. The other Hindus, though not externally accepted these stories, internally they felt sure of existence of them. In contrast to them the Christian and Muslim respondents neither asserted them nor denied them.

All the 271 Hindu respondents believed in 'papam' and 'punyam'. They had a different conception of the existence of heaven and hell. Thirty respondents believed in the existence of heaven and hell, whereas 90 respondents had an ambivalent attitude. According to 151 respondents there was nothing like heaven and hell separated, both are born out of one's own thinking and action. But 21 Christians and 8 Muslims believed in the existence of heaven and hell separately.

In respect of fate, 220 Hindu respondents believed in it hereas 51 did not. Both Christian and Muslim respondents onfirmed the existence of fate. So is also the case with belief and disbelief in magic. 266 Hindu respondents did not believe in magic, while 5 respondents confirmed their belief. All the Christian and Muslim respondents did not believe in magic since it has no religious and social sanction.

It may also be interesting to note that a great majority of 215 Hindu respondents felt equally religious with men, 30 more religious than men and 26 less religious than men. Christian and Muslim respondents confessed that they felt more or less religious with their men counterparts.

As regards fasting, 127 Hindu respondents sometimes, observed it, of them 74 respondents (58.3 per cent) for the longivity of their husbands, 23 (18.1 per cent) for purification of the body and 30 (23.6 per cent) for continuing traditional practice. Fasting is observed not only on particular festival days, but on any other day considered to be auspicious. But, 30 Brahmin repondents compulsorily observed fast on Vaikunta Ekadasi and Maha Sivarathri. It is, however, to be noticed that religious importance attached to fasting is slowly fading away.

Though all Hindu respondents did not observe and take part enthusiastically in local festivals such as the three Brahmostavams of three different temples, Lord Venkateswara of Tirumala, Lord Rama and Lord Govindaraja Swamy of Tirupati, they recognised the religious sanctity and importance. All the Hindu respondents had immense faith in Gangamma, the local Goddess. After the jatra is completed in the month of May, the respondents usually visit the Gangamma temple on any Friday or Tuesday. At the time of investigation 15 respondents had membership in religious organisations like International Institute of Krishna Conscience, Sathya Sai Seva Samiti, Hindu Dharma Prathisthapana and Ramakrishna Mission. They organised festivals, meetings and bhajans for propagating Hindu religion. On important religious gatherings, they served as volunteers. They attended the lectures addressed by spiritual leaders when they visited Tirupati town.

Members of the 15 joint-families adhered to many of the forms of Hindu worship, customs and practice. They had knowledge and feeling for them because the Hindu atmosphere reinforces a way of life. On important festivals and ceremonies, or auspicious days, every one of the family would take part and servants, family relations and caste community members would involve. This atmosphere it was found, was lacking in the nuclear families because of the absence of the contact with relatives, the presence of old family servants and lack of time as they were involved in occupations.

The Hindu working women, though they did not externally

observe various rituals and rites associated with festivals and ceremonies, they had firm belief in them. Their belief in Hinduism is undying. They maintain the feeling of oneness as it is based on the fact that Hindus understand each other through their religion. It is not the high philosophical basis of Hinduism but its popular manifestations that give one a sense of belonging to one another. In spite of the differences between Hindus, this gives them a common platform of understanding. Hinduism, according to them, is the basis of Hindu culture and it should not be lost.

With regard to the attitude of their children towards religious rituals and practices, the working women did not strictly impose and rub restrictions on them. But they still felt that their children were to be steeped in the atmosphere of Hindu belief. They maintained the home should reflect the spirit of religion. Individual worship was not enough. The worship was not confined to the altar but was the centre around which the household routine involved. Similarly, ceremonies and festivals were all interwoven with a pattern of life which had their sanctions from what is considered to be religious Dharma (duty) of the family. Unfortunately, this was no longer he basis of nuclear families among the respondents. This atmosphere was found lacking in their nuclear homes where there was neither the contact with relations or the presence of old family servants. The greatest preserver of traditional and customary religious practices was the joint family spirit. It was found absent. It may be further drawn that where the joint family sentiment was absent, it was almost felt impossible to transmit the feeling and faith rituals and symbols. Today, we see greater changes in the structure of family. The joint family has been replaced by the nuclear family. As a result several family values have undergone changes. The relationship between husband and wife and children and society has undergone radical transformation. In spite of knowing the significance of many rituals and their importance, it is no longer possible to incorporate them into the daily routine of their lives because the nuclear basis of the family is isolating and not conducive to the old discipline.

Several factors, as the author views, have contributed to the changes in the attitude of working women towards religious rituals and practices and beliefs. The most important have been advances in science and technology, national awareness and the changes in the social attitudes of women themselves with the widespread use of mass-media, besides modernisation, urbanisation and education. The shift from rural to urban living has also affected changes in the social roles of women.

Advances in science and technology have led to new production processes, occupations and skills which in turn created an increased demand for women labour. The spread of higher education paved the way for women to receive higher education in universities and professional colleges, resulting in many women having been highly qualified. They have gained access to increased employment opportunities vis-a-vis their higher education. Since women have been employed outside the homes, they are compelled to discharge two roles, the one is work role and the other family role. Thus, and employed house-wife is caught between her two roles. In the 'family role', a married women discharges the two roles, 'the mother' and 'the wife'. Besides, a house-wife performs other social obligations in relation to her parents, relatives and neighbours In addition to these activities associated with their family roles some of them are to perform another role, an occupational role, consisting of a number of activities. These two roles might require scheduling and rescheduling the time for them. Hence, we may say the performance of dual role by the working women might be the root cause for some changes witnessed in their religious practices and rituals.

Whatever the changes and the factors responsible for such changes might be, it is evidently proved beyond doubt from the information furnished by the respondents that though their adherence to religious rituals and practices was changed to some extent, their internal belief in some of them was not completely undermined and severely shaken. They still had immense faith in Hindu way of life. Their faith in religion was not destroyed. It is true they may have sacrificed certain customs and practices in view of the impact of certain environmental and institutional factors, but their deeply felt convictions and feelings were not destroyed. They still imbibed a greater spirit and inspiration from religion. They recognised the values drawn from religion. They particularly emphasised the existence of God in the universe. The fear of God and the fear of being punished for doing wrong things were over present among the working women.

Due to the necessity to work either for economic reasons or for intelletual satisfaction, the role of women has undergone a drastic change. This break is seen as most important and with far-reaching consequences. The perplexing question is whether it is possible for the modern, educated and employed woman to remain essentially committed to religious rituals and practices, traditions and values, to what extent these rituals and practices undergo changes in the future remain to be seen. The dilemma is how to take full advantage of modern opportunities without becoming western in outlook. The problem is in the process of modernisation, to what extent they maintain their way life and change on the foundations of their cultural values. However, it is of the author's view that whatever the possible changes that may take place in the practice of traditions, customs and beliefs, the working women are bound to firmly adhere to the religious tenets such as the existence of one God, divinity of the soul, the harmony of religions, the true basis for way of life, the non-duality of the God-Head and the unity of existence. Their faith in religion will never be shaken and destroyed.

Bibliography

Altekar, A.S. 1962 : *The Position of Women in Hindu Civilisation.*

Motilal Banarsidass, New Delhi.

Ajeet & Arpana Cour, 1976 : *Directory of Indian Women today* India Internationational Publications, New Delhi.

Asif Kidwai Mohammad, 1955 : *What Islam Is?* Printers and Printers, Lucknow.

Anjana Matra Sinha, 1993 : *Women in a changing Society* Ashish Publishing House, New Delhi.

Baig Tara Ali, 1958 : *Women of India.*

The Publications Division, Government of India, New Delhi.

Barth, A. 1978 : *The Religion of India.* Troby Rev, J. Wood, Light and Life Publications, New Delhi.

Bhushan, L.I. & Rambha Prasad 1993 ; *Concern for status among Educated Women.*

Classical Publishing Company, New Delhi.

Buck, C.H. 1977 : *Faiths, Fairs and Festivals of India* Asian Publication Service. New Delhi.

Boserup Esther 1970 : *Women's Role in Economic Development.* George Allen and Unwin Publications London.

Canney, M.A. 1976 : *An Encyclopaedia of Religions* Nag Publishers, New Delhi.

Chatterjee, S. 1950 : *The Fundamentals of Hinduism* Das Gupta and Company, Calcutta.

Chatterjee, S.N. 1968 : *A National outlook on Religion* Indian Books Distributors and Company, Calcutta.

Chaudhary, J. B. 1956 : *Women in Vedic Rituals* Pracyavani Publications, Calcutta.

Cormack, Margaret 1961 : *The Hindu Women* Asia Publishing House, Bombay.

De Souza Alfred 1980 : *Women in Contemporary India and South Asia.*

Manohar Publications, New Delhi.

Daran, D.V. 1981 : *Hinduism at a Glance*

United Printers Syndicate Pvt., Ltd., Madras.

Dubois, J.A. Abbe 1973 : *Hindu Manners, Customs and Ceremonies*

Mamta Publications, New Delhi.

Dutt, M.N. 1937 : *Status of Women* Mohendra Publishing Committee, Calcutta.

Deshpande, S.R. 1953 : *Economic and Social status of Women Workers in India*

Ministry of Labour, New Delhi.

Desai, Neera 1977 : *Women in Modern India* Vora and Company, Bombay.

Desai, Neera and Vibhuti Patel. 1985 : *Indian Women, Change and Challenge in the International decade 1975-1985*

Popular Prakashan, Bombay.

Everett Jana Matson 1979 : *Women and Social change in India* Heritage Publishers, New Delhi.

Farauhan: J.N. 1976 : *A Primer of Hinduism* Bharatiya Book Corporation, New Delhi.

Gadgil, D.R. 1965 : *Women in the Working force in India* Asia Publishing House, Bombay.

Gannep Arnold Van, 1960 : *The Rites of Passage.*
Routledge and Kegan Paul. London.

Ghosh, S.K. 1989 : *Indian Women through the ages.*
Ashish Publishing House, New Delhi.

Gupta, A.R. 1982 : *Women in Hindu Society.*
Jyotsna Prakashan. New Delhi.

Hastings, James 1918 : *Encyclopaedia of Religion and Ethics*
T & T Clark, Edinburgh.

Hate Chandrakala, A. 1969 : *Changing Status of Women.*
Allied Publishers Pvt., Ltd., New Delhi.

Hazra, R.C. 1975 ; *Studies in the Puranic Records on Hindu Rites and Customs*
Motilal Banarsi Dass, Delhi.

Hill Michael 1973 : *A Sociology of Religion.*
Heinemann Educational Books, London.

Jacobson J. & Wadley Susan 1977 : *Women in India : Two Perspectives.*
Manohar Book Service, New Delhi.

Jagadish Ayyar, P.V. 1982 : *South Indian Customs.*
Asian Educational Service, New Delhi.

Jessie, B. Tellis Nayak 1983 : *Indian Womenhood Then and Now.*
Satprakashan Sanchan Kendra, Indore.

Jogesa Chandra Ghosa, 1982 : *Hindu Women of India.*
Bimla Publishing House Ltd., New Delhi.

Jyotsna Chatterji, 1900 : *Religions and the Status of Momen*
Uppal Publishing House, New Delhi.

Kapadia, K.M. 1966 : *Marriage and Family in India*
Oxford University Press, Bombay.

Kapur Promilla, 1976 : *Marriage and Working Women in India.*
Vikas Publications, New Delhi.

Kane, P.V. 1947 : *History of the Dharmashastra : Ancient and Medieval Religious Civil Law in India. Vol. II*
Bhandarkar Oriental Research Institute. Pune.

Kidwai, Sheikh, M.H. 1978 : *Woman Under Different Social and Religious Laws.*
Light and Life Publishers, New Delhi.

Krishna Murthy, 1989 : *Women in Colonial India.*
Oxford University Press, New Delhi.

Lala Bajnath, R.B. 1981 : *Hinduism-Ancient and Modern*
Golden Publication Service, New Delhi.

Leech Maria and Jerome Fried, 1949 : *Dictionary of Folklore : Mythology and Legend*
Funk and Wagnalls Company, New York.

Mc Gasland, V Grace E, Cairns and David, C. Yu. 1969 : *Religions of the World.*
Random House. New York.

Madhavananda Swami 1953 : *Great Women of India.*
Advaite Ashrama, Mayavati.

Mahadevan T.M P. 1955 : *Outlines of Hinduism.*
Chetana Publishers, Bombay.

Monier Williams, M, 1971 : *Hinduism*
Rare Books, Delhi.

Morgan Kenneth, W. 1953 : *The Religions of the Hindus.*
The Ronald Press Company, New York

Manohar, K.M. 1983 : *Socio-Economic Status of Indian Women*
Seema Publications, Delhi.

Madhu Shastri 1990 : *Status of Hindu Women*
RBSA Publishers, Jaipur.

Narang Gokul Chand, 1966 : *Glorious Hinduism*
New Book Society of India, New Delhi.

Neera Desai & Maithreyi Krishna Raj 1990 : *Women and Society in India.*
Ajanta Publications, Delhi.

Padfield, J.E. 1975: *The Hindu at Home.*
B.R. Publishing Corporation, Delhi.

Pandey Raj Bali, 1976 : *Hindu Samskaras*
Motilal Banarsi Dass, New Delhi.

Patil Satyavrata 1980 : *Hinduism : Religion and Way of Life*
Associate Publishing House, New Delhi.

Phillips, M. 1903 : *The Evolution of Hinduism.*
M.E. Publishing House, Madras.

Phadnis Urmila & Indira Malini. 1978 : *Women of the World: Illusion and Reality.*
Vikas Publishing House Pvt. Ltd., New Delhi.

Paul Chowdhry 1992 : *Women Welfare and Development.*
Inter India Publications, New Delhi.

Radhakrishnan, S. 1971 : *The Hindu View of Life.*
George Allen and Unwin, Bombay.

Renou Louis 1961 : *Hinduism*
Prentice Hall, New York.

Rehana Ghadially 1988 : *Women in Indian Society*
Sage Publications, New Delhi.

Sarma, D.S. 1966 : *Renascent Hinduism.*
Bharatiya Vidya Bhavan, Bombay.

Sangeeta Mishra 1993 : *Status of Women in Changing Urban Hindu Family.*
Radha Publications, New Delhi.

Sharrock, John A. 1979 : *Hinduism-Ancient and Modern*
Bharatiya Publishing House, Delhi.

Saraswati Chennakesavan, 1974 : *A Critical Study of Hinduism*
Asia Publishing House, Bombay.

Sudha Gogate 1988 : *Status of Women.*
Shubhada Saraswat Prakasham. Pune.

Sushila Agrawal, 1988 : *Status of Momen*
Printwell Publishers, Jaipur.

Sushila Mehta, 1982 : *Revolution and Status of Women in India*
Metropolitan Book & Co., New Delhi.

Srinivas, M. N. 1978 : *The Changing Position of Indian Women*: Oxford University Press, New Delhi.

Subbamma Malladi, 1992 : *Hinduism and Women*. Ajanta Publications, Delhi.

Sills, L. David, 1968 : *International Encyclopaedia of Social Sciences Vol. V, VII, X and XII* Mac Millan Company and the Free Press.

Thomas, P. 1973 : *Epics, Myths and Legends of India*. D B. Taraporevala Sons & Company Pvt., Ltd., Bombay.

Turner, Victor, W. 1969 : *The Ritual Process* Routlege and Keganpaul, London.

Upadhaya Bhagwat Saran, 1974 : *Women in Rigveda* S. Chand & Co., New Delhi.

Weber Max 1967 : *The Religion of India* Mac Millian & Co., London.

Walker Benjamin, 1968 : *Hindu World* : *A Encyclopaedic Survey of Hinduism Vol. I*. George Allen and Unwin, London.

Index